Modern Critical Views

Modern Critical Views

Modern Critical Views

EUDORA WELTY

Edited and with an introduction by

Harold Bloom
Sterling Professor of the Humanities
Yale University

CHELSEA HOUSE PUBLISHERS
New York ◇ Philadelphia

Printed and bound in the United States of America

10 9 8 7 6 5 4

∞ The paper used in this publication meets the minimum
requirements of the American National Standard for
Permanence of Paper for Printed Library Materials, Z39.48-
1984.

Library of Congress Cataloging-in-Publication Data
Eudora Welty.
    (Modern critical views)
    Bibliography: p.
    Includes index.
    1. Welty, Eudora, 1909–   —Criticism and
interpretation—Addresses, essays, lectures.
I. Bloom, Harold.   II. Series.
PS3545.E6Z657   1986   813'.52   86-2582
ISBN 0-87754-718-1

Contents

Editor's Note

This book gathers together a representative selection of the most helpful criticism devoted to the fiction of Eudora Welty, arranged in the chronological order of its original publication. I am grateful to Nancy Sales for her aid in researching this volume.

The introduction centers upon two of Welty's stories, "A Still Moment " and "The Burning," in an attempt to isolate aspects of her rhetorical stance as a narrator. Katherine Anne Porter's tribute to the early stories in *A Curtain of Green* begins the chronological sequence, which continues with Robert Penn Warren's remarkable analysis of Welty's narrative vision, and with John Edward Hardy's reading of *Delta Wedding*'s regional symbolism. In some sense, Ruth M. Vande Kieft sums up the early critical approach to Welty by emphasizing how open the fiction holds itself to the mysteries and terrors of mere chance and oblivion, almost as though Welty maintains her humane stance gratuitously in a cosmos she knows might warrant only a nihilistic response.

Two distinguished novelists, Joyce Carol Oates and Reynolds Price, follow with accounts that confirm and extend this early judgment of Welty's art. Oates shrewdly compares Welty to Kafka as a writer who insists upon baffling our expectations, while Price gives a reading of the novella *The Optimist's Daughter*, in which we are made to see that Welty's first narrative stance, that of the onlooker, has been developed into a mode that now can conclude with a solitary joy.

Three gracious tributes—by Malcolm Cowley, Walker Percy, and Robert Penn Warren—are followed here by Cleanth Brooks's distinguished essay on the relation between Welty and the diverse Southern traditions, written and oral, that her best work mediates. A close analysis of *The Golden Apples* by Daniele Pitavy-Souques demonstrates how the book is structured according to three aspects of the myth of Perseus. Even subtler ingenuities of technique are explored in a reading of *Losing Battles* by Seymour Gross and in Michael Kreyling's account of pastoral symbolism in *The Robber Bridegroom*.

An interview with Welty conducted by Raad Cawthon provides an overview of the storyteller's indomitable humor and authentic cultural pride in her region's traditions. The final critical selection, by Patricia Meyer Spacks, adroitly balances the negative and positive uses of gossip in Welty's *Collected Stories* so as to leave us with another vision of Welty's heightened sense of community.

Introduction

I

Eudora Welty divides her remarkable brief autobiography, *One Writer's Beginnings*, into three parts: "Listening," "Learning to See," "Finding A Voice." Gentle yet admonitory, these titles instruct us in how to read her stories and novels, a reading that necessarily involves further growth in our sense of inwardness. Certain of her stories never cease their process of journeying deep into interior regions we generally reserve only for personal and experiential memories. Doubtless they differ from reader to reader; for me they include "A Still Moment" and "The Burning."

Mark Twain has had so varied a progeny among American writers that we hardly feel surprise when we reflect that Welty and Hemingway both emerge from *Huckleberry Finn*. All that Welty and Hemingway share as storytellers is Twain's example. Their obsessive American concern is Huck's: the freedom of a solitary joy, intimately allied to a superstitious fear of solitude. Welty's people, like Hemingway's, and like the self-representations of our major poets—Whitman, Dickinson, Stevens, Frost, Eliot, Hart Crane, R. P. Warren, Roethke, Elizabeth Bishop, Ashbery, Merrill, and Ammons—all secretly believe themselves to be no part of the creation and all feel free only when they are quite alone.

In *One Writer's Beginnings*, Welty comments upon "A Still Moment":

> "A Still Moment"—another early story—was a fantasy, in which the separate interior visions guiding three highly individual and widely differing men marvelously meet and converge upon the same single exterior object. All my characters were actual persons who had lived at the same time, who would have been strangers to one another, but whose lives had actually taken them at some point to the same neighborhood. The scene was in the Mississippi wilderness in the historic year 1811—*"anno mirabilis,"* the year

1

the stars fell on Alabama and lemmings, or squirrels perhaps, rushed straight down the continent and plunged into the Gulf of Mexico, and an earthquake made the Mississippi River run backwards and New Madrid, Missouri, tumbled in and disappeared. My real characters were Lorenzo Dow the New England evangelist, Murrell the outlaw bandit and murderer on the Natchez Trace, and Audubon the painter; and the exterior object on which they all at the same moment set their eyes is a small heron, feeding.

Welty's choices—Lorenzo Dow, James Murrell, Audubon—are all obsessed solitaries. Dow, the circuit rider, presumably ought to be the least solipsistic of the three, yet his fierce cry as he rides on at top speed—"I must have souls! And souls I must have!"—is evidence of an emptiness that never can be filled:

> It was the hour of sunset. All the souls that he had saved and all those he had not took dusky shapes in the mist that hung between the high banks, and seemed by their great number and density to block his way, and showed no signs of melting or changing back into mist, so that he feared his passage was to be difficult forever. The poor souls that were not saved were darker and more pitiful than those that were, and still there was not any of the radiance he would have hoped to see in such a congregation.

As Dow himself observes, his eyes are in a "failing proportion to my loving heart always," which makes us doubt his heart. He loves his wife, Peggy, effortlessly since she is in Massachusetts and he is galloping along on the Old Natchez Trace. Indeed, their love can be altogether effortless, consisting as it does of a marriage proposal, accepted as his first words to her, a few hours of union, and his rapid departure south for evangelical purposes, pursued by her first letter declaring that she, like her husband, fears only death, but never mere separation.

This remarkable hunter of souls, intrepid at evading rapacious Indians or Irish Catholics, can be regarded as a sublime lunatic, or merely as a pure product of America:

> Soon night would descend, and a camp-meeting ground ahead would fill with its sinners like the sky with its stars. How he hungered for them! He looked in prescience with a longing of love over the throng that waited while the flames of the torches threw change, change, change over their faces. How could he

bring them enough, if it were not divine love and sufficient warning of all that could threaten them? He rode on faster. He was a filler of appointments, and he filled more and more, until his journeys up and down creation were nothing but a shuttle, driving back and forth upon the rich expanse of his vision. He was homeless by his own choice, he must be everywhere at some time, and somewhere soon. There hastening in the wilderness on his flying horse he gave the night's torch-lit crowd a premature benediction, he could not wait. He spread his arms out, one at a time for safety, and he wished, when they would all be gathered in by his tin horn blasts and the inspired words would go out over their heads, to brood above the entire and passionate life of the wide world, to become its rightful part.

He peered ahead. "Inhabitants of Time! The wilderness is your souls on earth!" he shouted ahead into the treetops. "Look about you, if you would view the conditions of your spirit, put here by the good Lord to show you and afright you. These wild places and these trails of awesome loneliness lie nowhere, nowhere, but in your heart."

Dow is his own congregation, and his heart indeed contains the wild places and awesomely lonesome trails through which he endlessly rushes. His antithesis is provided by the murderous James Murrell, who suddenly rides at Dow's side, without bothering to look at him. If Dow is a mad angel, Murrell is a scarcely sane devil, talking to slow the evangelist down, without realizing that the sublimely crazy Lorenzo listens only to the voice of God:

Murrell riding along with his victim-to-be, Murrell, riding, was Murrell talking. He told away at his long tales, with always a distance and a long length of time flowing through them, and all centered about a silent man. In each the silent man would have done a piece of evil, a robbery or a murder, in a place of long ago, and it was all made for the revelation in the end that the silent man was Murrell himself, and the long story had happened yesterday, and the place *here*—the Natchez Trace. It would only take one dawning look for the victim to see that all of this was another story and he himself had listened his way into it, and that he too was about to recede in time (to where the dread was forgotten) for some listener and to live for a listener in the long ago. Destroy the present!—that must have been the first thing that was whispered in Murrell's heart—the living moment and the man that lives in it must die before you can go on. It was his habit to bring the journey—which might even take days—to a close with a kind of ceremony. Turning his face at last into the face of the victim, for he had never seen him before now, he would tower up with the sudden height of a man no longer the tale teller but the speechless protagonist, silent at last, one degree nearer the hero. Then he would murder the man.

Since Murrell is capable of observing nothing whatsoever, he does not know what the reader knows, which is that Lorenzo is not a potential victim for this self-dramatizing Satanist. Whatever the confrontation between angel and devil might have brought (and one's surmise is that Murrell might not have survived), the crucial moment is disturbed by the arrival of a third, the even weirder Audubon:

Audubon said nothing because he had gone without speaking a word for days. He did not regard his thoughts for the birds and animals as susceptible, in their first change, to words. His long playing on the flute was not in its origin a talking to himself. Rather than speak to order or describe, he would always draw a deer with a stroke across it to communicate his need of venison to an Indian. He had only found words when he discovered that there is much otherwise lost that can be noted down each item in its own day, and he wrote often now in a journal, not wanting anything to be lost the way it had been, all the past, and he would write about a day, "Only sorry that the Sun Sets."

These three extraordinarily diverse obsessives share a still moment, in which "a solitary snowy heron flew down not far away and began to feed beside the marsh water." To Lorenzo, the heron's epiphany is God's love become visible. To Murrell, it is "only whiteness ensconced in darkness," a prophecy of the slave, brigand, and outcast rebellion he hopes to lead in the Natchez country. To Audubon it is precisely what it is, a white heron he must slay if he is to be able to paint, a model that must die in order to become a model. Welty gives us no preference among these three:

What each of them had wanted was simply *all*. To save all souls, to destroy all men, to see and record all life that filled this world— all, all—but now a single frail yearning seemed to go out of the three of them for a moment and to stretch toward this one snowy, shy bird in the marshes. It was as if three whirlwinds had drawn together at some center, to find there feeding in peace a snowy heron. Its own slow spiral of flight could take it away in its own time, but for a little it held them still, it laid quiet over them, and they stood for a moment unburdened. . . .

To quest for *all* is to know anything but peace, and "a still moment" is only shared by these three questers in a phantasmagoria. When the moment ends with Audubon's killing of the bird, only Lorenzo's horrified reaction is of deep import or interest. Murrell is content to lie back in ambush and await travelers more innocent, who will suit his Satanic destiny as Lorenzo and Audubon could not. Audubon is also content to go on, to fulfill his vast design. But Lorenzo's epiphany has turned into a negative moment and though he will go on to gather in the multitudes, he has been darkened:

> In the woods that echoed yet in his ears, Lorenzo riding slowly looked back. The hair rose on his head and his hands began to shake with cold, and suddenly it seemed to him that God Himself, just now, thought of the Idea of Separateness. For surely He had never thought of it before, when the little white heron was flying down to feed. He could understand God's giving Separateness first and then giving Love to follow and heal in its wonder; but God had reversed this, and given Love first and then Separateness, as though it did not matter to Him which came first. Perhaps it was that God never counted the moments of Time; Lorenzo did that, among his tasks of love. Time did not occur to God. Therefore—did He even know of it? How to explain Time and Separateness back to God, Who had never thought of them, Who could let the whole world come to grief in a scattering moment?

This is a meditation on the verge of heresy, presumably Gnostic, rather than on the border of unbelief. Robert Penn Warren, in a classical early essay on "Love and Separateness in Eudora Welty" (1944), reads the dialectic of Love and Separateness here as the perhaps Blakean contraries of Innocence and Experience. On this reading, Welty is an ironist of limits and of contamination, for whom knowledge destroys love, almost as though love could survive only upon enchanted ground. That may underestimate both Lorenzo and Welty. Pragmatically, Lorenzo has been unchanged by the still moment of love and its shattering into separateness; indeed he is as unchanged as Murrell or Audubon. But only Lorenzo remains haunted by a vision, by a *particular* beauty greater than he can account for, and yet never can deny. He *will* change some day, though Welty does not pursue that change.

II

The truth of Welty's fictive cosmos, for all her preternatural gentleness, is that love always does come first, and always does yield to an irreparable separateness. Like her true mentor, Twain, she triumphs in comedy because her deepest awareness is of a nihilistic "unground" beyond consciousness or metaphysics, and comedy is the only graceful defense against that cosmological emptiness. Unlike Faulkner and Flannery O'Connor, she is, by design, a genial writer, but the design is a subtler version of Twain's more urgent desperation. "A Still Moment," despite its implications, remains a fantasy of the continuities of quest. Rather than discuss one of her many masterpieces of humorous storytelling, I choose instead "The Burning," which flamboyantly displays her gift for a certain grim sublimity, and which represents her upon her heights, as a stylist and narrator who can rival Hemingway in representing the discontinuities of war and disaster.

"The Burning" belongs to the dark genre of Southern Gothic, akin to Faulkner's "A Rose for Emily" and O'Connor's "A Good Man Is Hard to Find." Welty, as historical a storyteller as Robert Penn Warren, imagines an incident from Sherman's destructive march through Georgia. The imagining is almost irrealistic in its complexity of tone and indirect representation, so that "The Burning" is perhaps the most formidable of all Welty's stories, with the kind of rhetorical and allusive difficulties we expect to encounter more frequently in modern poetry than in modern short stories. Writing on form in D. H. Lawrence's stories, Welty remarked on "the unmitigated shapelessness of Lawrence's narrative" and sharply noted that his characters would only appear deranged if they began to speak on the streets as they do in the stories:

> For the truth seems to be that Lawrence's characters don't really speak their words—not conversationally, not to one another—they are *not* speaking on the street, but are playing like fountains or radiating like the moon or storming like the sea, or their silence is the silence of wicked rocks. It is borne home to us that Lawrence is writing of our human relationships on earth in terms of eternity, and these terms set Lawrence's form. The author himself appears in authorship in places like the moon, and sometimes smites us while we stand there under him.

The characters of Welty's "The Burning" fit her description of Lawrence's men and women; their silence too is the silence of wicked rocks. Essentially they are only three: two mad sisters, Miss Theo and Miss Myra, and their slave, called Florabel in the story's first published version (*Harper's Bazaar*, March, 1951). The two demented high-born ladies are very different; Miss Theo is deep-voiced and domineering, Miss Myra gentler and dependent. But little of the story is seen through their eyes or refracted through either's consciousness. Florabel, an immensely passive being, sees and reacts, in a mode not summarized until nearly the end of the story, in its first printed form:

> Florabel, with no last name, was a slave. By the time of that moment on the hill, her kind had been slaves in a dozen countries and that of their origin for thousands of years. She let everything be itself according to its nature—the animate, the inanimate, the symbol. She did not move to alter any of it, not unless she was told to and shown how. And so she saw what happened, the creation and the destruction. She waited on either one and served it, not expecting anything of it but what she got; only sooner or later she would seek protection somewhere. Herself was an unknown, like a queen, somebody she had heard called, even cried for. As a slave she was earth's most detached visitor. The world had not touched her—only possessed and hurt her, like a man; taken away from her, like a man; turned another way from her and left her, like a man. Her vision was clear. She saw what was there and had not sought it, did not seek it yet. (It was *her* eyes that were in the back of her head, her vision that met itself coming the long way back, unimpeded, like the light of stars.) The command to loot was one more fading memory. Many commands had been given her, some even held over from before she was born; delayed and miscarried and interrupted, they could yet be fulfilled, though it was safer for one once a slave to hear things a second time, a third, fourth, hundredth, thousandth, if they were to be carried out to the letter. In that noon quiet after conflict there might have been only the two triumphant, the mirror which was a symbol in the world and Florabel who was standing there; it was the rest that had died of it.

The mirror, "a symbol in the world," is in this first version of "The Burning" a synecdoche for the fragmented vision of both mad sisters and their slave. In rewriting the story, Welty uses the mirror more subtly. Delilah (as Florabel is now named) sees Sherman's soldiers and their apocalyptic white horse directly as they enter the house, and she runs to tell Miss Theo and Miss Myra. They deign to look up and observe the intruders in the mirror over the fireplace. Throughout the rest of the catastrophic narrative, the sisters behold everything that transpires as though in a mirror. Clearly they have spent their lives estranging reality as though looking in a mirror, and they move to their self-destruction as though they saw themselves only as images. The violence that prepares for the burning is thus rendered as phantasmagoria:

> The sisters showed no surprise to see soldiers and Negroes alike (old Ophelia in the way, talking, talking) strike into and out of the doors of the house, the front now the same as the back, to carry off beds, tables, candlesticks, washstands, cedar buckets, china pitchers, with their backs bent double; or the horses ready to go; or the food of the kitchen bolted down—and so much of it thrown away, this must be a second dinner; or the unsilenceable dogs, the old pack mixed with the strangers and fighting with all their hearts over bones. The last skinny sacks were thrown on the wagons—the last flour, the last scraping and clearing from Ophelia's shelves, even her pepper-grinder. The silver Delilah could count was counted on strange blankets and then, knocking against the teapot, rolled together, tied up like a bag of bones. A drummer boy with his drum around his neck caught both Miss Theo's peacocks, Marco and Polo, and wrung their necks in the yard. Nobody could look at those bird-corpses; nobody did.

The strangling of the peacocks is a presage of the weirdest sequence in "The Burning," in which Miss Theo and Miss Myra hang themselves from a tree, with Delilah assisting as ordered. It is only when the sisters are dead that we begin to understand that "The Burning" is more Delilah's story than it ever could have been theirs. A baby, Phinny, who had been allowed to perish in the fire (Welty does not allow us to know why), turns out to have been begotten by Miss Theo's and Miss Myra's brother Benton upon Delilah:

> The mirror's cloudy bottom sent up minnows of light to the brim where now a face pure as a water-lily shadow was floating. Almost too small and deep down to see, they were quivering, leaping to life, fighting, aping old things Delilah had seen done in this world already, sometimes what men had done to Miss Theo and Miss Myra and the peacocks and to slaves, and sometimes what a slave had done and what anybody now could do to anybody. Under the flicker of the sun's licks, then under its whole blow and blare, like an unheard scream, like an act of mercy gone, as the wall-

less light and July blaze struck through from the opened sky, the mirror felled her flat.

She put her arms over her head and waited, for they would all be coming again, gathering under her and above her, bees saddled like horses out of the air, butterflies harnessed to one another, bats with masks on, birds together, all with their weapons bared. She listened for the blows, and dreaded that whole army of wings—of flies, birds, serpents, their glowing enemy faces and bright kings' dresses, that banner of colors forked out, all this world that was flying, striking, stricken, falling, gilded or blackened, mortally splitting and falling apart, proud turbans unwinding, turning like the spotted dying leaves of fall, spiraling down to bottomless ash; she dreaded the fury of all the butterflies and dragonflies in the world riding, blades unconcealed and at point—descending, and rising again from the waters below, down under, one whale made of his own grave, opening his mouth to swallow Jonah one more time.

Jonah!—a homely face to her, that could still look back from the red lane he'd gone down, even if it was too late to speak. He was her Jonah, her Phinny, her black monkey; she worshiped him still, though it was long ago he was taken from her the first time.

Delilah, hysterical with fear, shock, and anguish, has fallen into the mirror world of the mad sisters, her self-slain mistresses. She is restored to some sense of reality by her search for Phinny's bones. Carrying them, and what she can save of the sisters' finery, she marches on to what is presented ambiguously either as her own freedom, or her death, or perhaps both together:

Following the smell of horses and fire, to men, she kept in the wheel tracks till they broke down at the river. In the shade underneath the burned and fallen bridge she sat on a stump and chewed for a while, without dreams, the comb of a dirtdauber. Then once more kneeling, she took a drink from the Big Black, and pulled the shoes off her feet and waded in.

Submerged to the waist, to the breast, stretching her throat like a sunflower stalk above the river's opaque skin, she kept on, her treasure stacked on the roof of her head, hands laced upon it. She had forgotten how or when she knew, and she did not know what day this was, but she knew—it would not rain, the river would not rise, until Saturday.

This extraordinary prose rises to an American sublime that is neither grotesque nor ironic. Welty, in her *On Short Stories*, asked the question: "Where does beauty come from, in the short story?" and answered only that beauty was a result:

> It *comes*. We are lucky when beauty comes, for often we try and it should come, it could, we think, but then when the virtues of our story are counted, beauty is standing behind the door.

I do not propose to count the virtues of "The Burning," or even of "A Still Moment." Both narratives are as thoroughly written through, fully composed, as the best poems of Wallace Stevens or of Hart Crane, or the strongest of Hemingway's stories, or Faulkner's *As I Lay Dying*. American writing in the twentieth century touches the sublime mode only in scattered instances, and always by reaching the frontier where the phantasmagoric, and the realism of violence, are separated only by ghostlier demarcations, keener sounds. Welty's high distinction is that in her the demarcations are as ghostly, the sounds as keen, as they are in her greatest narrative contemporaries, Faulkner and Hemingway.

KATHERINE ANNE PORTER

A Curtain of Green

Friends of us both first brought Eudora Welty to visit me three years ago in Louisiana. It was hot midsummer, they had driven over from Mississippi, her home state, and we spent a pleasant evening together talking in the cool old house with all the windows open. Miss Welty sat listening, as she must have done a great deal of listening on many such occasions. She was and is a quiet, tranquil-looking, modest girl, and unlike the young Englishman of the story, she has something to be modest about, as this collection of short stories proves.

She considers her personal history as hardly worth mentioning, a fact in itself surprising enough, since a vivid personal career of fabulous ups and downs, hardships and strokes of luck, travels in far countries, spiritual and intellectual exile, defensive flight, homesick return with a determined groping for native roots, and a confusion of contradictory jobs have long been the mere conventions of an American author's life. Miss Welty was born and brought up in Jackson, Mississippi, where her father, now dead, was president of a Southern insurance company. Family life was cheerful and thriving; she seems to have got on excellently with both her parents and her two brothers. Education, in the Southern manner with daughters, was continuous, indulgent, and precisely as serious as she chose to make it. She went from school in Mississippi to the University of Wisconsin, thence to Columbia, New York, and so home again where she lives with her mother, among her lifelong friends and acquaintances, quite simply and amiably. She tried a job or two because that seemed the next thing, and did some publicity and

From *A Curtain of Green*. © 1941 by Eudora Welty. Doubleday Publishing Co., 1941. Originally entitled "Introduction."

newspaper work; but as she had no real need of a job, she gave up the notion and settled down to writing.

She loves music, listens to a great deal of it, all kinds; grows flowers very successfully, and remarks that she is "underfoot locally," meaning that she has a normal amount of social life. Normal social life in a medium-sized Southern town can become a pretty absorbing occupation, and the only comment her friends make when a new story appears is, "Why, Eudora, when did you write that?" Not how, or even why, just when. They see her about so much, what time has she for writing? Yet she spends an immense amount of time at it. "I haven't a literary life at all," she wrote once, "not much of a confession, maybe. But I do feel that the people and things I love are of a true and human world, and there is no clutter about them. . . . I would not understand a literary life."

We can do no less than dismiss that topic as casually as she does. Being the child of her place and time, profiting perhaps without being aware of it by the cluttered experiences, foreign travels, and disorders of the generation immediately preceding her, she will never have to go away and live among the Eskimos, or Mexican Indians; she need not follow a war and smell death to feel herself alive: she knows about death already. She shall not need even to live in New York in order to feel that she is having the kind of experience, the sense of "life" proper to a serious author. She gets her right nourishment from the source natural to her—her experience so far has been quite enough for her and of precisely the right kind. She began writing spontaneously when she was a child, being a born writer; she continued without any plan for a profession, without any particular encouragement, and, as it proved, not needing any. For a good number of years she believed she was going to be a painter, and painted quite earnestly while she wrote without much effort.

Nearly all the Southern writers I know were early, omnivorous, insatiable readers, and Miss Welty runs reassuringly true to this pattern. She had at arms's reach the typical collection of books which existed as a matter of course in a certain kind of Southern family, so that she had read the ancient Greek and Roman poetry, history and fable. Shakespeare, Milton, Dante, the eighteenth-century English and the nineteenth-century French novelists, with a dash of Tolstoy and Dostoievsky, before she realized what she was reading. When she first discovered contemporary literature, she was just the right age to find first W. B. Yeats and Virginia Woolf in the air around her; but always, from the beginning until now, she loved folk tales, fairy tales, old legends, and she likes to listen to the songs and stories of people who live in old communities whose culture is recollected and bequeathed orally.

She has never studied the writing craft in any college. She has never belonged to a literary group, and until after her first collection was ready to be published she had never discussed with any colleague or older artist any problem of her craft. Nothing else that I know about her could be more satisfactory to me than this; it seems to me immensely right, the very way a young artist should grow, with pride and independence and the courage really to face out the individual struggle; to make and correct mistakes and take the consequences of them, to stand firmly on his own feet in the end. I believe in the rightness of Miss Welty's instinctive knowledge that writing cannot be taught, but only learned, and learned by the individual in his own way, at his own pace and in his own time, for the process of mastering the medium is part of a cellular growth in a most complex organism; it is a way of life and a mode of being which cannot be divided from the kind of human creature you were the day you were born, and only in obeying the law of this singular being can the artist know his true directions and the right ends for him.

Miss Welty escaped, by miracle, the whole corrupting and destructive influence of the contemporary, organized tampering with young and promising talents by professional teachers who are rather monotonously divided into two major sorts: those theorists who are incapable of producing one passable specimen of the art they profess to teach; or good, sometimes first-rate, artists who are humanly unable to resist forming disciples and imitators among their students. It is all well enough to say that, of this second class, the able talent will throw off the master's influence and strike out for himself. Such influence has merely added new obstacles to an already difficult road. Miss Welty escaped also a militant social consciousness, in the current radical-intellectual sense, she never professed Communism, and she has not expressed, except implicitly, any attitude at all on the state of politics or the condition of society. But there is an ancient system of ethics, an unanswerable, indispensable moral law, on which she is grounded firmly, and this, it would seem to me, is ample domain enough; these laws have never been the peculiar property of any party or creed or nation, they relate to that true and human world of which the artist is a living part; and when he dissociates himself from it in favor of a set of political, which is to say, inhuman, rules, he cuts himself away from his proper society—living men.

There exist documents of political and social theory which belong, if not to poetry, certainly to the department of humane letters. They are reassuring statements of the great hopes and dearest faiths of mankind and they are acts of high imagination. But all working, practical political systems, even those professing to originate in moral grandeur, are based upon and operate by contempt of human life and the individual fate; in accepting any one of them and shaping his mind and work to that mold, the artist dehumanizes himself, unfits himself for the practise of any art.

Not being in a hurry, Miss Welty was past twenty-six years when she offered her first story, "The Death of a Traveling Salesman," to the editor of a little magazine unable to pay, for she could not believe that anyone would buy a story from her; the magazine was *Manuscript*, the editor John Rood, and he accepted it gladly. Rather surprised, Miss Welty next tried the *Southern Review*, where she met with a great welcome and the enduring partisanship of Albert Erskine, who regarded her as his personal discovery. The story was "A Piece of News" it was followed by others published in the *Southern Review*, the *Atlantic Monthly*, and *Harper's Bazaar*.

She has, then, never been neglected, never unappreciated, and she feels simply lucky about it. She wrote to a friend: "When I think of Ford Madox Ford! You remember how you gave him my name and how he tried his best to find a publisher for my book of stories all that last year of his life; and he wrote me so many charming notes, all of his time going to his little brood of promising writers, the kind of thing that could have gone on forever. Once I read in the *Saturday Review* an article of his on the species and the way they were neglected by publishers, and he used me as the example chosen at random. He ended his cry with 'What is to become of both branches of Anglo-Saxondom if this state of things continues?' Wasn't that wonderful, really, and typical? I may have been more impressed by that than would other readers who knew him. I did not know him, but I knew it was typical. And here I myself have turned out to be not at all the martyred promising writer, but have had all the good luck and all the good things Ford chided the world for withholding from me and my kind."

But there is a trap lying just ahead, and all short-story writers know what it is—The Novel. That novel which every publisher hopes to obtain from every short-story writer of any gifts at all, and who finally does obtain it, nine times out of ten. Already publishers have told her, "Give us first a novel, and then we will publish your short stories." It is a special sort of trap for poets, too, though quite often a good poet can and does write a good novel. Miss Welty has tried her hand at novels, laboriously, dutifully, youthfully thinking herself perhaps in the wrong to refuse, since so many authoritarians have told her that was the next step. It is by no means the next step. She can very well become a master of the short story, there are almost perfect stories in this book. It is quite possible she can never write a novel, and there is no reason why she should. The short story is a special and difficult medium, and contrary to a widely spread popular superstition it has no formula that can be taught by correspondence school. There is nothing to hinder her from writing novels if she wishes or believes she can. I only say that her good gift, just as it is now, alive and flourishing, should not be retarded by a perfectly artificial demand upon her to do the conventional thing. It is a fact that the public for short stories is smaller than the public for novels; this seems to me no good reason for depriving that minority. I remember a reader writing to an editor, complaining that he did not like collections of short stories because, just as he had got himself worked into one mood or frame of mind, he was called upon to change to another. If that is an important objection, we might also apply it to music. We might compare the novel to a symphony, and a collection of short stories to a good concert recital. In any case, this complainant is not our reader, yet our reader does exist, and there would be more of him if more and better short stories were offered.

These stories offer an extraordinary range of mood, pace, tone, and variety of material. The scene is limited to a town the author knows well; the farthest reaches of that scene never go beyond the boundaries of her own state, and many of the characters are of the sort that caused a Bostonian to remark that he would not care to meet them socially. Lily Daw is a half-witted girl in the grip of social forces represented by a group of earnest ladies bent on doing the best thing for her, no matter what the consequences. Keela, the Outcast Indian Maid, is a crippled little Negro who represents a type of man considered most unfortunate by W. B. Yeats: one whose experience was more important than he, and completely beyond his powers of absorption. But the really unfortunate man in this story is the ignorant young white boy, who had innocently assisted at a wrong done the little Negro, and for a most complex reason, finds that no reparation is possible, or even desirable to the victim. . . . The heroine of "Why I Live at the P. O." is a terrifying case of dementia praecox. In this first group—for the stories may be loosely classified on three separate levels—the spirit is satire and the key grim comedy. Of these, "The Petrified Man" offers a fine clinical study of vulgarity—vulgarity absolute, chemically pure, exposed mercilessly to its final subhuman depths. Dullness, bitterness, rancor, self-pity, baseness of all kinds, can be most interesting material for a story provided these are not also the main elements in the mind of the author. There is nothing in the least vulgar or frustrated in Miss Welty's mind. She has simply an eye and an ear sharp, shrewd, and true as a tuning fork. She has given to this little story all her wit and observation, her blistering humor and her just cruelty; for she has none of that slack tolerance or sentimental tenderness toward symptomatic evils that amounts to criminal collusion between author and character. Her use of this material raises the quite awfully sordid little tale to a level above its natural habitat, and its realism seems almost to have the quality of caricature, as complete realism so often does. Yet, as painters of the grotesque make only detailed reports of actual living types observed more keenly than the average eye is capable of observing, so Miss Welty's little human monsters are not really caricatures at all, but individuals exactly and clearly presented: which is perhaps a case against realism, if we cared to go into it. She does better on another level—for the important reason that the themes are richer—in such beautiful stories as "Death of a Traveling Salesman," "A Memory," "A Worn Path." Let me admit a deeply personal preference for this particular kind of story, where external act and the internal voiceless life of the human imagination almost meet and mingle on the mysterious threshold between dream and waking, one reality refusing to admit or confirm the existence of the other, yet both conspiring toward the same end. This is not easy to accomplish, but it is always worth trying, and Miss Welty is so successful at it, it would seem her most familiar territory. There is no blurring at the edges, but evidences of an active and disciplined imagination working firmly in a strong line of continuity, the waking faculty of daylight reason recollecting and recording the crazy logic of the dream. There is in none of these stories any trace of autobiography in the prime sense, except as the author is omnipresent, and knows each character she writes about as only the artist knows the thing he has made, by first experiencing it in imagination. But perhaps in "A Memory," one of the best stories, there might be something of early personal history in the story of the child on the beach, alienated from the world of adult knowledge by her state of childhood, who hoped to learn the secrets of life by looking at everything, squaring her hands before her eyes to bring the observed thing into a frame—the gesture of one born to select, to arrange, to bring apparently disparate elements into harmony within deliberately fixed boundaries. But the author is freed already in her youth from self-love, self-pity, self-preoc-cupation, that triple damnation of too many of the young and gifted, and has reached an admirable objectivity. In such stories as "Old Mr. Marble-hall," "Powerhouse," "The Hitch-Hikers," she combines an objective re-porting with great perception of mental or emotional states, and in "Clytie" the very shape of madness takes place before your eyes in a straight account of actions and speech, the personal appearance and habits of dress of the main character and her family.

In all of these stories, varying as they do in excellence, I find nothing false or labored, no diffusion of interest, no wavering of mood—the approach is direct and simple in method, though the themes and moods are anything but simple, and there is even in the smallest story a sense of power in reserve which makes me believe firmly that, splendid beginning that this is, it is only the beginning.

> But now that so much is being changed, is it not time that we should change? Could we not try to develop ourselves a little, slowly and gradually take upon ourselves our share in the labor of love? We have been spared all its hardship . . . we have been spoiled by easy enjoyment. . . . But what if we despised our successes, what if we began from the beginning to learn the work of love which has always been done for us? What if we were to go and become neophytes, now that so much is changing?
>
> (Rilke)

ROBERT PENN WARREN

Love and Separateness in Eudora Welty

*He could understand God's giving Separateness first and then giving Love to
follow and heal in its wonder; but God had reversed this, and given Love first
and then Separateness, as though it did not matter to Him which came first.*
                                                            —"A Still Moment"

If we put *The Wide Net*, Eudora Welty's second collection of stories, up
against her first collection, *A Curtain of Green*, we can immediately observe
a difference: the stories of *The Wide Net* represent a specializing, an intensifying, of one of the many strains which were present in *A Curtain of Green*.
All of the stories in *A Curtain of Green* bear the impress of Miss Welty's
individual talent, but there is a great variety among them in subject matter
and method and, more particularly, mood. It is almost as if the author had
gone at each story as a fresh start in the business of writing fiction, as if she
had had to take a new angle each time out of a joy in the pure novelty of
the perspective. We find the vindictive farce of "The Petrified Man," the
nightmare of "Clytie," the fantasy and wit of "Old Mr. Marblehall," the
ironic self-revelation of "Why I Live at the P.O.," the nearly straight realism
of "The Hitch-Hikers," the macabre comedy and pathos of "Keela, the
Outcast Indian Maiden." The material of many of the stories was sad, or
violent, or warped, and even the comedy and wit were not straight, but if
read from one point of view, if read as a performance, the book was exhil-
arating, even gay, as though the author were innocently delighted not only
with the variety of the world but with the variety of ways in which one
could look at the world and the variety of things that stories could be and
still be stories. Behind the innocent delight of the craftsman, and of the

From *Selected Essays*. © 1958 by Robert Penn Warren. Random House, 1958.

admirer of the world, there was also a seriousness, a philosophical cast of mind, which gave coherence to the book, but on the surface there was the variety, the succession of surprises. In *The Wide Net* we do not find the surprises. The stories are more nearly cut to one pattern.

We do not find the surprises. Instead, on the first page, with the first sentence of the first story, "First Love," we enter a special world: "Whatever happened, it happened in extraordinary times, in a season of dreams . . ." And that is the world in which we are going to live until we reach the last sentence of the last story. "Whatever happened," the first sentence begins, as though the author cannot be quite sure what did happen, cannot quite undertake to resolve the meaning of the recorded event, cannot, in fact, be too sure of recording all of the event. This is coyness, of course; or a way of warning the reader that he cannot expect quite the ordinary direct light on the event. For it is "a season of dreams"—and the faces and gestures and events often have something of the grave retardation, the gnomic intensity, the portentous suggestiveness of dreams. The logic of things here is not quite the logic by which we live, or think we live, our ordinary daylight lives. In "The Wide Net," for example, the young husband, who thinks his wife has jumped into the river, goes out with a party of friends to dredge for the body, but the sad occasion turns into a saturnalian fish-fry which is interrupted when the great King of the Snakes raises his hoary head from the surface of the river. But usually, in *The Wide Net*, the wrenching of logic is not in terms of events themselves, though "The Purple Hat" is a fantasy, and "Asphodel" moves in the direction of fantasy. Usually the events as events might be given a perfectly realistic treatment (Dreiser could take the events of "The Landing" for a story). But in these cases where the events and their ordering are "natural" and not supernatural or fantastic, the stories themselves finally belong to the "season of dreams" because of the special tone and mood, the special perspective, the special sensibility with which they are rendered.

Some readers, in fact, who are quite aware of Miss Welty's gifts, have recently reported that they are disturbed by the recent development of her work. Diana Trilling, in her valuable and sobering comments on current fiction, which appear regularly in the *Nation*, says that the author "has developed her technical virtuosity to the point where it outweighs the uses to which it is put, and her vision of horror to the point of nightmare." There are two ideas in this indictment, and let us take the first one first and come to the second much later. The indictment of the technique is developed along these lines: Miss Welty has made her style too fancy—decorative, "falsely poetic" and "untrue," "insincere." ("When an author says 'look at me' instead of 'look at it,' there is insincerity.") This insincerity springs from "the extreme infusion of subjectivism and private sensibility." But the subjectivism, Mrs. Trilling goes on to say, leads not only to insincerity and fine writing but to a betrayal of the story's obligation to narrative and rationality. Miss Welty's stories take off from a situation, but "the stories themselves stay with their narrative no more than a dance, say, stays with its argument." That is the summary of the indictment.

The indictment is, no doubt, well worth the close attention of Miss Welty's admirers. There is, in fact, a good deal of the falsely poetic in Miss Welty's present style, metaphors that simply pretend to an underlying logic, and metaphors (and descriptions) that, though good themselves, are irrelevant to the business in hand. And sometimes Miss Welty's refusal to play up the objective action—her attempt to define and refine the response rather than to present the stimulus—does result in a blurred effect. But the indictment treats primarily not of such failures to fulfill the object the artist has set herself but of the nature of that object. The critic denies, in effect, that Miss Welty's prresent kind of fiction is fiction at all: "It is a book of ballets, not of stories."

Now is it possible that the critic is arguing from some abstract definition of "story," some formalistic conception which does not accommodate the present exhibit, and is not concerning herself with the question of whether or not the present exhibit is doing the special job which it proposes for itself, and, finally, the job which we demand of all literature? Perhaps we should look at a new work first in terms of its effect and not in terms of a definition of type, because every new work is in some degree, however modest, wrenching our definition, straining its seams, driving us back from the formalistic definition to the principles on which the definition was based. Can we say this, therefore, of our expectation concerning a piece of literature, new or old: That it should intensify our awareness of the world (and of ourselves in relation to the world) in terms of an idea, a "view." This leads us to what is perhaps the key statement by Diana Trilling concerning *The Wide Net*: she grants that the volume "has tremendous emotional impact, despite its obscurity." In other words, she says, unless I misinterpret her, that the book does intensify the reader's awareness—but *not* in terms of a presiding idea.

This has led me to reread Miss Welty's two volumes of stories in the attempt to discover the issues which are involved in the "season of dreams." To begin with, almost all of the stories deal with people who, in one way or another, are cut off, alienated, isolated from the world. There is the girl in "Why I Live at the P.O."—isolated from her family by her arrogance, meanness, and sense of persecution; the half-witted Lily Daw, who, despite the efforts of "good" ladies, wants to live like other people; the deaf-mutes of "The Key," and the deaf-mute of "First Love"; the people of "The Whistle" and "A Piece of News," who are physically isolated from the world and who make their pathetic efforts to re-establish something lost; the traveling salesman and the hitch-hikers of "The Hitch-Hikers," who, for their different reasons, are alone, and the traveling salesman of "Death of a Traveling Salesman" who, in the physically and socially isolated backwoods cabin, discovers that he is the one who is truly isolated; Clytie, isolated in family pride and madness and sexual frustration, and Jenny of "At the Landing," and Mrs. Larkin of "A Curtain of Green," the old women of "A Visit of Charity" and the old Negro woman of "A Worn Path"; the murderer of "Flowers for Marjorie," who is cut off by an economic situation and the pressure of a great city; Mr. Marblehall in his secret life; Livvie, who, married to an old man and trapped in his respectable house, is cut off from the life appropriate to her years; Lorenzo, Murrell, and Audubon in "A Still Moment," each alone in his dream, his obsession; the old maids of "Asphodel," who tell the story of Miss Sabina and then are confronted by the naked man and pursued by the flock of goats. In some of the cases, the matter is more indirectly presented. For instance, in "Keela, the Outcast Indian Maiden," we find, as in *The Ancient Mariner*, the story of a man who, having committed a crime, must try to re-establish his connection with humanity; or in the title story of *The Wide Net*, William Wallace, because he thinks his wife has drowned herself, is at the start of the story cut off from the world of natural joy in which he had lived.

We can observe that the nature of the isolation may be different from case to case, but the fact of isolation, whatever its nature, provides the basic situation of Miss Welty's fiction. The drama which develops from this basic situation is of either of two kinds: first, the attempt of the isolated person to escape into the world; or second, the discovery by the isolated person, or by the reader, of the nature of the predicament.

As an example of the first type, we can remember Clytie's obsessed inspection of faces ("Was it possible to comprehend the eyes and the mouth of other people, which concealed she knew not what, and secretly asked for still another unknown thing?") and her attempt to escape, and to solve the mystery, when she lays her finger on the face of the terrified barber who has come to the ruinous old house to shave her father. Or there is Jenny, of "At the Landing," or Livvie, or the man of "Keela." As an example of the second type, there is the new awareness on the part of the salesman in "The Hitch-Hikers," or the new awareness on the part of the other salesman in the back-country cabin.

Even in "A Still Moment" we have this pattern, though in triplicate. The evangelist Lorenzo, the outlaw Murrell, and the naturalist and artist Audubon stand for a still moment and watch a white heron feeding. Lorenzo sees a beauty greater than he can account for (he had earlier "accounted for" the beauty by thinking, "Praise God, His love has come visible"), and with the sweat of rapture pouring down from his forehead, shouts into the marshes, "Tempter!" He has not been able to escape from his own obsession, or in other words, to make his definition of the world accommodate the white heron and the "natural" rapture which takes him. Murrell, looking at the bird, sees "only whiteness ensconced in darkness," and thinks that "if it would look at him a dream penetration would fill and gratify his heart"— the heart which Audubon has already defined as belonging to the flinty darkness of a cave. Neither Lorenzo nor Murrell can "love" the bird, and so escape from their own curse as did, again, the Ancient Mariner. But there remains the case of Audubon himself, who does "love" the bird, who can innocently accept nature. There is, however, an irony here. To paint the bird he must "know" the bird as well as "love" it, he must know it feather by feather, he must have it in his hand. And so he must kill it. But having killed the bird, he knows that the best he can make of it now in a painting would be a dead thing, "never the essence, only a sum of parts," and that "it would always meet with a stranger's sight, and never be one with beauty in any other man's head in the world." Here, too, the fact of the isolation is realized: as artist and lover of nature he had aspired to a communication, a communion, with other men in terms of the bird, but now "he saw his long labor most revealingly at the point where it met its limit" and he is forced back upon himself.

"A Still Moment," however, may lead us beyond the discussion of the characteristic situation, drama, and realization in Miss Welty's stories. It may lead us to a theme which seems to underlie the stories. For convenience, though at the risk of incompleteness, or even distortion, we may call it Innocence and Experience. Let us take Audubon in relation to the heron. He loves the bird, innocently, in its fullness of being. But he must subject this love to knowledge; he must kill the bird if he is to commemorate its beauty, if he is to establish his communion with other men in terms of the bird's beauty. There is in the situation an irony of limit and contamination.

Let us look at this theme in relation to other stories. "A Memory," in *A Curtain of Green*, gives a simple example. Here we have a young girl lying on a beach and looking out at the scene through a frame made by her fingers, for the girl can say of herself, "To watch everything about me I regarded grimly and possessively as a need." (As does Audubon, in "A Still Moment.")

And further: "It did not matter to me what I looked at; from any observation I would conclude that a secret of life had been nearly revealed to me. . . ." Now the girl is cherishing a secret love, a love for a boy at school about whom she knows nothing, to whom she has never even spoken, but whose wrist her hand had once accidentally brushed. The secret love had made her watching of the world more austere, had sharpened her demand that the world conform to her own ideas, and had created a sense of fear. This fear had seemed to be realized one day when, in the middle of a class, the boy had a fit of nosebleed. But that is in the past. This morning she suddenly sees between the frame of her fingers a group of coarse, fat, stupid, and brutal people disporting themselves on the sand with a maniacal, aimless vigor which comes to climax when the fat woman, into the front of whose bathing suit the man had poured sand, bends over and pulls down the cloth so that the lumps of mashed and folded sand empty out. "I felt a peak of horror, as though her breasts themselves had turned to sand, as though they were of no importance at all and she did not care." Over against this defilement (a defilement which implies that the body, the breasts which turn to sand, has no meaning), there is the refuge of the dream, "the undefined austerity of my love."

"A Memory" presents the moment of the discovery of the two poles— the dream and the world; the idea and nature; innocence and experience; individuality and the anonymous, devouring life-flux; meaning and force; love and knowledge. It presents the contrast in terms of horror (as do "The Petrified Man" and "Why I Live at the P.O." when taken in the context of Miss Welty's work) and with the issue left in suspension, but other stories present it with different emphases and tonalities.

For instance, when William Wallace, in "The Wide Net," goes out to dredge the river, he is presumably driven by the fear that his wife has jumped in, but the fear is absorbed into the world of the river, and in a saturnalian revel he prances about with a great catfish hung on his belt, like a river-god laughing and leaping. But he had also dived deep down into the water: "Had he suspected down there, like some secret, the real true trouble that Hazel had fallen into, about which words in a letter could not speak . . . how (who knew?) she had been filled to the brim with that elation that they all remembered, like their own secret, the elation that comes of great hopes and changes, sometimes simply of the harvest time, that comes with a little course of its own like a tune to run in the head, and there was nothing she could do about it, they knew—and so it had turned into this? It could be nothing but the old trouble that William Wallace was finding out, reaching and turning in the gloom of such depths."

This passage comes clear when we recall that Hazel, the wife who is supposed to have commited suicide by drowning, is pregnant: she had sunk herself in the devouring life-flux, has lost her individuality there, just as the men hunting for the body have lost the meaning of their mission. For the river is simply force, which does not have its own definition; in it are the lost string of beads to wind around the little Negro boy's head, the catfish for the feast, the baby alligator that looks "like the oldest and worst lizard," and the great King of the Snakes, As Doc, the wise old man who owns the net, says: "The outside world is full of endurance." And he also says: "The excursion is the same when you go looking for your sorrow as when you go looking for your joy." Man has the definition, the dream, but when he plunges into the river he runs the risk of having it washed away. But it is important to notice that in this story, there is not horror at the basic contrast, but a kind of gay acceptance of the issue: when William Wallace gets home he finds that his wife had fooled him, and spanks her, and then she lies smiling in the crook of his arm. "It was the same as any other chase in the end."

As "The Wide Net," unlike "A Memory," does more than merely present the terms of contrast, so do such stories as "Livvie" and "At the Landing." Livvie, who lives in the house of wisdom (her infirm husband's name is Solomon) and respectability (the dream, the idea, which has withered) and Time (there is the gift of the silver watch), finally crosses into the other world, the world of the black buck, the field hand, in his Easter clothes—another god, not a river-god but a field god. Just after Solomon's death, the field hand in his gorgeous Easter clothes takes Livvie in his arms, and she drops the watch which Solomon had given her, while outside "the redbirds were flying and crisscrossing, the sun was in all the bottles on the prisoned trees, and the young peach was shining in the middle of them with the bursting light of spring."

If Livvie's crossing into the world of the field god is joyous, the escape of Jenny, in "At the Landing," is rendered in a different tonality. This story assimilates into a new pattern many of the elements found in "A Memory," "The Wide Net," "Livvie," and "Clytie." As in the case of Clytie, Jenny is caught in the house of pride, tradition, history, and as in the case of Livvie, in a house of death. The horror which appears in "A Memory," in "Clytie," reappears here. The basic symbolism of "Livvie" and of "The Wide Net" is again called into play. The river, as in "The Wide Net," is the symbol of that world from which Jenny is cut off. The grandfather's dream at the very beginning sets up the symbolism which is developed in the action:

"The river has come back. That Floyd came to tell me. The sun was shining full on the face of the church, and that Floyd came around it with his wrist hung with a great long catfish. . . . That

Floyd's catfish has gone loose and free. . . . And all of a sudden, my dears—my dears, it took its river life back, and shining so brightly swam through the belfry of the church, and downstream."

Floyd, the untamed creature of uncertain origin, is like William Wallace, the river-god dancing with the great catfish at his belt. But he is also, like the buck in "Livvie," a field god, riding the red horse in a pasture full of butterflies. He is free and beautiful, and Jenny is drawn after him, for "she knew that he lived apart in delight." But she also sees him scuffling playfully with the hideous old Mag: the god does not make nice distinctions. When the flood comes over the Landing (upsetting the ordered lives, leaving slime in the houses), Floyd takes her in his boat to a hill (significantly the cemetery hill where her people are buried), violates her, feeds her wild meat and fish (field and river), and when the flood is down, leaves her. She has not been able to talk to him, and when she does say, "I wish you and I could be far away. I wish for a little house," he only stares into the fire as though he hasn't heard a word. But after he has gone she cannot live longer in the Landing; she must find him.

Her quest leads her into the dark woods (which are like an underwater depth) and to the camp of the wild river people, where the men are throwing knives at a tree. She asks for Floyd, but he is not there. The men put her in a grounded houseboat and come in to her. "A rude laugh covered her cry, and somehow both the harsh human sounds could easily have been heard as rejoicing, going out over the river in the dark night." Jenny has crossed into the other world to find violence and contamination, but there is not merely the horror as in "Clytie" and "A Memory." Jenny has acted out a necessary role: she has moved from the house of death, like Livvie, and there is "gain" as well as "loss." We must not forget the old woman who looks into the dark houseboat, at the very end of the story, and understands when she is told that the strange girl is "waiting for Billy Floyd." The old woman nods "out to the flowing river, with the firelight following her face and showing its dignity."

If this general line of interpretation is correct, we find that the stories represent variations on the same basic theme, on the contrasts already enumerated. It is not that there is a standard resolution for the contrasts which is repeated from story to story; rather, the contrasts, being basic, are not susceptible of a single standard resolution, and there is an implicit irony in Miss Welty's work. But if we once realize this, we can recognize that the contrasts are understood not in mechanical but in vital terms: the contrasts

provide the terms of human effort, for the dream must be carried to, submitted to, the world, innocence to experience, love to knowledge, knowledge
to fact, individuality to communion. What resolution is possible is, if I read
the stories with understanding, in terms of the vital effort. The effort is a
"mystery," because it is in terms of the effort, doomed to failure but essential,
that the human manifests itself as human. Again and again, in different
forms, we find what we find in Joel of "First Love": "Joel would never know
now the true course, or the true outcome of any dream: this was all he felt.
But he walked on, in the frozen path into the wilderness, on and on. He
did not see how he could ever go back and still be the boot-boy at the Inn."

It is possible that, in trying to define the basic issue and theme of Miss
Welty's stories, I have made them appear too systematic, too mechanical. I
do not mean to imply that her stories should be read as allegories, with a
neat point-to-point equating of image and idea. It is true that a few of her
stories, such as "The Wide Net," do approach the limit of allegory, but even
in such cases we find rather than the system of allegory a tissue of symbols
which emerge from, and disappear into, a world of scene and action which,
once we discount the author's special perspective, is recognizable in realistic
terms. The method is similar to the method of much modern poetry, and
to that of much modern fiction and drama, but at the same time it is a method
as old as fable, myth, and parable. It is a method by which the items of
fiction (scene, action, character, etc.) are presented not as document but as
comment, not as a report but as a thing made, not as history but as idea.
Even in the most realistic and reportorial fiction, the social picture, the
psychological analysis, and the pattern of action do not rest at the level of
mere report; they finally operate as expressive symbols as well.

Fiction may be said to have two poles, history and idea, and the emphasis
may be shifted very far in either direction. In the present collection the
emphasis has been shifted very far in the direction of idea, but at the same
time there remains a sense of the vividness of the actual world: the picnic
of "The Wide Net" is a real picnic as well as a "journey," Cash of "Livvie"
is a real field hand in his Easter clothes as well as a field god. In fact, it may
be said that when the vividness of the actual world is best maintained, when
we get the sense of one picture superimposed upon another, different and
yet somehow the same, the stories are most successful.

The stories which fail are stories like "The Purple Hat" and "Asphodel,"
in which the material seems to be manipulated in terms of an idea, in which
the relation between the image and the vision has become mechanical, in
which there is a strain, in which we do find the kind of hocus-pocus deplored
by Diana Trilling.

And this brings us back to the criticism that the volume "has tremendous emotional impact, despite its obscurity," that the "fear" it engenders is "in inverse ratio to its rational content." Now it seems to me that this description does violence to my own experience of literature, that we do not get any considerable emotional impact unless we sense, at the same time, some principle of organization, some view, some meaning. This does not go to say that we have to give an abstract formulation to that principle or view or meaning before we can experience the impact of the work, but it does go to say that it is implicit in the work and is having its effect upon us in immediate aesthetic terms. Furthermore, in regard to the particular work in question, I do not feel that it is obscure. If anything, the dreamlike effect in many of the stories seems to result form the author's undertaking to squeeze meaning from the item which, in ordinary realistic fiction, would be passed over with a casual glance. Hence the portentousness, the retardation, the otherworldliness. For Miss Welty is like the girl in "A Memory":

> from any observation I would conclude that a secret of life had been nearly revealed to me, and from the smallest gesture of a stranger I would wrest what was to me a communication or a presentiment.

In many cases, as a matter of fact, Miss Welty has heavily editorialized her fiction. She wants us to get that smallest gesture, to participate in her vision of things as intensely meaningful. And so there is almost always a gloss to the fable.

One more word: it is quite possible that Miss Welty has pushed her method to its most extreme limit. It is also possible that the method, if pursued much farther, would lead to monotony and self-imitation and merely decorative elaboration. Perhaps we shall get a fuller drama when her vision is submitted more daringly to fact, when the definition is plunged into the devouring river. But meanwhile Miss Welty has given us stories of brilliance and intensity; and as for the future, Miss Welty is a writer of great resourcefulness, sensitivity, and intelligence, and can probably fend for herself.

JOHN EDWARD HARDY

Delta Wedding *as Region and Symbol*

The reputation of Eudora Welty is beginning to outrun criticism of her work. We need something comprehensive in the way of a study, something less hasty than the review and something at once more objective and not so essentially condescending as the *bon voyage* essay. Wherever it was she was going, I think it will be generally agreed that Miss Welty has by now arrived—perhaps for the second or third time—and it would be no longer very discerning to treat the seasoned traveler as if she were the young Isabel Archer.

But, such is the nature of her work itself, a study that is to be really comprehensive must be most particular. We will have to take one thing— or one thing at a time, anyway. The Welty reader too should be lessoned with the characterizing refrain-phrase of E. M. Forster's little essay on Virginia Woolf—"one thing—one." And the one thing I want to consider here is *Delta Wedding*. A great many critics seem to think that Miss Welty is at her best in the shorter forms; and perhaps she feels so too, to judge from the continued emphasis of her work. But this novel, it seems to me, is not only still the biggest thing, but still the most rigidly restricted, disciplined. It has most characteristically developed that sense of the symbolic particularity of things, of a place and a time and people, which can make the good regionalist the most universal of artists—or of novelists, at any rate. It is the most "one"—whole.

I mean to suggest, then, that the most important thing about the novel is its formal structure. But if the nature of its design has, perhaps, escaped many readers, the reasons are not hard to find. There is considerable prej-

From *The Sewanee Review* 60, no. 3 (Summer 1952). © 1952, 1980 by the University of the South.

udice against a "serious" novelist's treating material of this kind with such an attitude of sympathy as Miss Welty assumes. Certainly it was obvious from the start, to a reader with any sensitivity at all, that *Delta Wedding* was not simply another Mississippi plantation, "historical" novel, designed for a bosom-and-columns dust jacket. But, if the author's irony is felt from the first sentence, its essence is very subtle. And the patience of a good many of the liberal reviewers a few years ago was pretty short.

If Miss Welty wasn't starry-eyed in quite the usual way about "the South," she wasn't indignant either, or even decently tough and realistic now and again. She had distinctly her own version of what Wyndham Lewis called Faulkner's "whippoorwill tank"; but it might have seemed only unfortunately less manageable than his. The novel *was*, after all, historical— that its time was only about twenty and not seventy-five or a hundred years past was calculated to allay suspicion only slightly. Few eyebrows were raised particularly over the treatment of the Negroes in the novel; but they might well have been. The darkies were sometimes just a little too charmingly typical. And where the attitude went beyond one of placid acceptance—this remains, I think, one of the most genuinely distressing flaws of the novel— it often became only half-heartedly apologetic, with a rather strong suggestion of the old "well, at least they had *status*" routine. What Miss Welty could do with Negroes at her best in some of the short stories seemed rather sadly absent here. And one could go only so far in justifying it on grounds of dramatic propriety, that the author was bound to the point-of-view of the white characters of the story; simply for purposes of realism, it might easily have been made a little *more* apparent how severely restricted that outlook was in this regard.

And yet the immediate inferences from all this are, clearly, not correct. And perhaps the best way of getting at *why* they are not correct is simply to allow the novel to establish for itself the perspective in which we are to look at its features.

One has first to see that Miss Welty is not taking *any* attitude toward "the South." The story is about the Delta, at the most—not the South, not even Mississippi. Yankees, of course, are unthinkable; but Ellen, the Virginian, is acutely conscious all her life of *her* difference from the Delta family she mothers. And the circle is drawn even closer; Troy Flavin, who is largely responsible for the significance of the wedding as a symbol of threatened disruption, is alien by virtue of being a *hill-country* Mississippian. And (disregarding for the moment Laura McRaven, whose case is rather special), Robbie Reid, whom the family wisely regard as a far greater threat to the insularity of their world even than Troy, is foreign as a native of the *town* of Fairchilds, as distinguished from the plantation.

The psychological basis of the relationship of the characters one to another here is simple enough, of course. The barrier between Robbie Reid and the Fairchilds is greatest for several reasons—simply that she is a woman, that she is the unworthy wife of the darling of the family, but most important of all, that she *is* a lifelong near neighbor. In any society, of course, class distinctions are always, though ironically, most keenly appreciated by native members of the immediate community. Troy Flavin, not so much out of mere stupidity as simply because his origins are more remote, finds nothing so terribly formidable in the family he is "marrying into"—as he puts it with a confidence which dismays and amuses those who know the Fairchilds. And in the face of his naïve assurance, the family are fairly constrained to be gentle with him, though they make little effort to hide their feelings from Dabney. But the point I want to make just now is that this narrowing of the circle is carried so far that it finally excludes emphasis upon the kind of typicality, the true provincialism, in character and situation, which is characteristic of the commonplace regional novel. The Fairchilds are finally most typical, if at all, in their very singularity. And it is at this point that the principle of exclusiveness almost ceases, or for the reader's purposes in understanding the novel ought almost to cease, to be social principle at all. It becomes, rather, the *formal* principle, and the principle of sensibility, in a version of pastoral which has been before only vaguely hinted at in the Southern novel.

Miss Welty's awareness of the classic elements of pastoral in the situation she is dealing with is quite evident. One may take as an initial statement of the conventional "paradox" of pastoral, the familar principle of inversion of values, one of Laura's early reflections—"Jackson was a big town, with twenty-five thousand people, and Fairchilds was just a store and a gin and a bridge and one big house, yet she was the one who felt like a little country cousin when she arrived."

But it is just the awareness it reveals which is most important about a passage like this. What it says, the statement of the pastoral "formula" in these terms, is only a starting point. The tradition of the Southern novel has been all but exclusively pastoral from the start, of course—and in a great many different ways, both naturalistic and romantic. But there has been before no such fully *conscious* exploring of the implications of the mode as Miss Welty's, an insight which finally carries beyond the significance of the form for the *mores* of the society which produced it.

(Something of this sort—its wit, its merging of realism and magic, its delicacy, its formal and elegiac ironies, its universal mythiness, and basic to all the rest its struggle between anonymity and self-consciousness—is inevitable toward the *end* of any cycle of pastoral. And the reader might well

have to go back to the Sixteenth and Seventeenth centuries of English literature for instructive parallels.)

Miss Welty's depiction of the Delta society and its structure, of the
family as the typical unit of that society, is studiedly accurate, right, always
in substance and, with the exception of a few distressing lapses into an over-
precious style, nearly always in tone. The rightness of it meets the test of
communication certainly even to the reader unfamiliar with the actuality.
And the structure of the society, in the pattern of the novel as well as in
fact, clearly produces and supports the kind of hyperdeveloped individuality
which the characters severally manifest. But it is one of the basic paradoxes
of the novel—one of which several of the characters are keenly aware—that
the strength of the society to support is entirely the dynamic of the personality's constant and tireless struggle with it. And the center of interest, finally,
is in the exercise of entirely private sensibilities—not so much in the relationships abstractly as such among the various people, as in the way in which
each person privately *sees* those relationships.

Indeed, at the beginning of the novel, and again qualifiedly at the end,
it is not even people and their relationships which are *seen*—but *things*, rather.
Laura comes into the Delta country with the bemused aloneness of the
adventurer into an enchanted forest. Other people, as people, are secondary
realities—the signs of their existence, to the extent that she is aware of them
at all, becoming talismans of a significance entirely private to her, the ticket
she had stuck in her hat band, "in imitation of the drummer across the aisle."
It is things that are most alive—the fields, the train itself becoming a creature
of the fields. And then the train "seemed to be racing with a butterfly."

The vision is not quite ecstatic. The sun which in its sinking momen-
tarily obliterates the most basic distinction—"all that had been bright or dark
was now one color"—is a real sun. It sinks, and Laura arrives, and is met
by the Fairchild cousins, real, other people. The last word on Laura before
the conductor cries "Fairchilds!" is simply that she "felt what an arriver in
a land feels." And though there has been fair warning that the land is to be
much more than *a* land—"the clouds were large . . . larger than anything
except the fields the Fairchilds planted"; "the Delta buzzards . . . seemed to
wheel as high and wide as the sun"; "the west was a milk-white edge, like
the foam of the sea"—it is only a warning so far. There is no immediate
plunge to that depth of the private consciousness in which the particular
becomes the universal. If the reader constructs a cloud-cuckoo-land here, it
is his own doing. Miss Welty has no unrealistic intention of giving away her
story in one lyric offering. Certain pertinent, practical facts stick in Laura's
mind. She knows where she came from and where she is going and why.

She is conscious of time—and her reality in it—she has been here before. (The fact that the visit, to "nature," out of the life of the city, is a *return*, functions similarly to the same fact in Wordsworth's *Tintern Abbey*, for example.) Even in her vision of the immensity of the clouds it is not just the fields that they are compared to, but the fields "that the Fairchilds planted." The fields belong to them, and not simply as a matter of economics either, we are soon to discover. The myth is theirs too. The train was a legendary creature, it had its name of the Yellow Dog, in *their* consciousness before hers. Their baffling otherness, their exclusiveness and possessiveness, threatens both to invade and to shut her out at every level of her sensibility.

But what we do get in this opening passage is just enough of the ecstatic to reassure us that Laura's personal emotional problem doesn't *matter* a great deal. (The reader is never permitted actually to "feel sorry" for Laura; the "poor Laura, little motherless girl" greeting which she anticipates has only a ritualistic solemnity, no real sadness.) And, conversely, we are assured that the personal "problems" of the others aren't going to matter a great deal either—which, in turn, is further assurance on Laura's account. We get, in other words, the symbolic sense—we begin to see things with a great, though not quite a whole, measure of aesthetic distance. (This, by the way, accounts I think for the time-setting of the novel. Aside from the fact that the early Twenties actually were a period of significant social and economic transition—the slight, but only slight, removal in time makes it easier for the author to put the emphasis just where she wants it, upon probability rather than upon the kind of mere possibility which our generation demands not only of the immediately contemporary novel but of the usual historical one as well.) The action takes on from the beginning, and never quite loses, even at the highest pitch of visual excitement, the somewhat cool, formal tone of the conscious pastoral.

One feels from the beginning that it is not actions, but reactions, which are to count. A few things do manage to happen in the course of the novel—Dabney and Troy do marry, Robbie comes back to George, it is decided that Laura will stay at Shellmound, at least for a time. But this is not a great deal, after all. And—the marriage is the most obvious example—it is perfectly clear that none of these things is of great moment in itself. The word "wedding" in the title is important. It is in a sense with the wedding, the ritual, not the marriage, that Miss Welty is concerned. The ritual sense is private, of course; the ceremony itself is passed over in a few words—"Mr. Rondo married Dabney and Troy." Mr. Rondo's status, the status of the church in the Fairchild world, perfectly defines the more than baronial self-sufficiency of the family, their superiority to any larger public, institutional significance of their affairs. But, private both in the sense that the family has its peculiar rituals and even more in the sense that each individual has his own in which the others do not participate, it is ritual nonetheless. There are no raw emotions in the novel—and little of a structure of personal involvements, conflicts, as we have observed, about the center of a "problem" which is carried through to some resolution in action. Nor is it that the story is actionless simply in the sense of being introspective—with much private examination of motives, intentions, much logical self-analysis. No one has time for much introspection in this usual sense. There is, in fact, a great deal *going on* all the time. But the incidents are important mainly as points of refraction, from which light is cast back upon various moments of symbolic perception in the minds of the several characters.

This is where Miss Welty is at her best, and where one has to start looking for the "meaning" of the novel, in the whole particularity of the moment, the single, illuminating, still act of private *perception*. It is where one has to look for the truth about the characters, severally. They don't communicate much of themselves to one another, however much they are in a sense involved with one another, and mutually dependent.

The thing is stated over and over again, this impregnable, at times reassuring, at times to one or another hopelessly baffling, privacy of the consciousness of every person, of the being of every thing which the consciousness entertains, even of every separate *moment* of consciousness. There are the various lights, with the obvious significance of light, especially of light *inside* something. The lamp which the aunts give to Dabney, a *night-light*, notably, itself an object of family tradition but, given to Dabney, becoming the prime symbol of her independence, her private rebellion of indifference when she carelessly breaks it, carrying out the theme of general disaster which the very flame itself, the intended source of light and comfort, draws out upon the shade—"The picture on it was a little town. Next, in the translucence over the little town with trees, towers, people, windowed houses, and a bridge, over the clouds and stars and moon and sun, you saw a redness glow and the little town was all on fire, even to the motion of fire, which came from the candle flame drawing." The same lamp in India's perception, precious and cherished, but in infinite secrecy, and so again a symbol of impenetrable isolation, the magic circle of her privacy—"India made a circle with her fingers, imagining she held the little lamp"—the vessel of light filled, paradoxically, "with the mysterious and flowing air of night." The light on the back porch, when Shelley comes in alone for a moment away from the dancers, and "the moths spread upon the screens, the hard beetles knocked upon the radius of light like an adamant door," as she falls

into musing; the light in her room, as she sits writing in her diary, with the
beetle again clawing at the screen.

The various places of hiding and retreat. The seemingly innumerable
rooms of the house itself. The wood in which Ellen walks, with its mysteriously ageless, directionless paths. The privilege, if it is a privilege
altogether, is denied not even to the Negroes. Partheny, in the chinaberry-
hidden fastness of her house in Brunswicktown, retiring into the undisturbed,
unquestioned and unanswerable, mystery of her "mindlessness." Aunt Studney, with her jealously guarded sack that is to the children perhaps the
source of life itself, the place where babies come from—her very existence
hardly more, as the reader is permitted to perceive it, than a legendary
creation of the family's very love of the eternal secret, than the name which
puns her one, uncommunicative phrase—"Ain't studyin' you."

Or simply the sudden, isolated moments of private illumination. Dabney's ride in the morning, when she sees Marmion, sees it first *reflected* in
the river, "and then the house itself reared delicate and vast, with a strict
tower, up from its reflection," sees it defiantly and exultantly alone, "while
they never guessed, she had seen Marmion . . . all had been before her eyes
when she was all by herself." The loneliness of Laura, abandoned during
the game of hide-and-seek, in which she perceives the necessity of George's
isolation. "Then she saw Uncle George walk out of the house and stare out
into the late day. She wanted to call out to him, but . . . something told her
. . . that it was right for him to stand apart, and that when he opened an
envelope in a room no one should enter. Now she felt matter-of-factly intimate with it, with his stand and his predicament."

Or, more definitive still, the sound of Mary Lamar Mackey's piano—
the constant music which is a figure of the author's omnipresence, proceeding
from an all but invisible source (we get only one brief close-up of Mary
Lamar), only now and again distinctly heard at some chance pause in the
activity, but always there. At a moment of tense silence during the first
hours of Robbie's visit, Mary Lamar "was playing a nocturne—like the
dropping of rain or the calling of a bird the notes came from another room,
effortless and endless, isolated from them, yet near, and sweet like the
guessed existence of mystery. It made the house like a nameless forest,
wherein many little lives lived privately, each to its lyric pursuit and shy
protection. . ." The momentary perfection of the pastoral vision.

And it is this sort of thing, of course, that gives the novel its first
appearance of disorder. The characters seem hopelessly unpredictable, their
actions unmotivated and obscure, without intelligible issue; the transitions,
from one scene to another, from the reflections of one character to another,

appear entirely capricious. It would seem at first glance that Miss Welty has sacrificed an order of the whole entirely in the interest of an illusion of life in the details. But it ought to be apparent from the very symbols, and symbolic instances, of the privacy of consciousness given here, that there is order of a kind. The lives, the thoughts, of all the characters are intensely private—but because they are ritualistic too, and ritual is always inevitable, they fall into patterns which transcend the privacy, with or without the consciousness of the particular character. And, if the characters themselves are not often conscious of the pattern, the author is clearly conscious of it. It emerges, beyond its inevitability, as a principle of deliberate and controlled artistry, in an order of *recurrence* which informs the whole action of the novel. The order of the novel is a poetic order—of recurrent themes, symbols, and motives of symbolic metaphor. And it must be close-read, as a poem.

Perhaps the thread nearest the center of the design is that of the story, told and re-told, again and again reflected upon and alluded to, of George and Maureen on the railroad trestle. Certain reasons for the importance of the story to the Fairchilds are immediately apparent. It was just after the incident on the trestle that Troy and Dabney had "gone on up the railroad track and got engaged"—thus beginning the latest threat to the solidarity of the Fairchild world. It was then that Robbie Reid, providing the climax to the story with her accusation, "George Fairchild, you didn't do this for *me*!," brought into the open the whole complex of bitter feelings which the Fair- childs entertain for this earlier, and even more significant than Dabney's, "bad match"—their resentment at the love of poor, common little Robbie for George, George who is the universally acknowledged, living embodiment of their ideal of Fairchild man, their infuriated amusement at her daring to intrude the voice of her "rights" even against his defense of what is even more holy to the Fairchilds than George or any *living* thing, the memory of the dead Denis. Robbie's thinking of herself at that moment, her indignation at George's willingness to sacrifice himself for the semi-idiotic Maureen, defines perfectly for the Fairchild *women* especially her hopeless failure to understand their vision of themselves—and their investment of that vision in Denis, of whom nothing remains but his daughter Maureen, the crazy Virgie Lee, a few vague stories and a little pathetic "poetry," but who in their minds is the more dignified by the "tragedy" of indignities, and who finally is beyond reproach (as even George cannot be) simply by virtue of being dead, who as the symbol of the holy past is worthy of *any* sacrifice. Robbie's behavior at the trestle is all of a piece with the absurdity, the hopeless childishness, of her taunt that the Fairchilds are "not even rich!"— her failure to comprehend the myth of their aristocracy.

This much, then—beyond what is simply their love, aristocratically both pious and hilariously irreverent, for a *story*, any story, which involves the family—all the Fairchilds understand, in one way or another. They understand also something of how important it is that the train was the familiar Yellow Dog, the train that is almost itself their property—so that it *could not* actually have killed George (thus the whole thing became absurd enough for amusement), and yet, faithful servitor, provides enough of the thrill of danger, of death, for the purposes of their ritual.

Ellen, who retains enough of the attitude of an outsider always to see (or to have to see, to figure out consciously) a little more than the others, understands also what it meant for Robbie—she is a little daunted, even, seeing that Robbie has had a vision, a vision of *fact*, that makes the Fairchilds' prattling over their legend a little ridiculous. She understands that a train on that track *can* kill, that it has killed the astonishingly beautiful girl she met in the woods, and that if her daughters are spared it is only perhaps because they are *not* that beautiful, not beautiful enough to be heroines of a genuine tragedy. And she understands, finally, George's role in all of it. In a way that no one else can be, because no one else knows about the lost girl, she is at once both grateful and ashamed at the implications of George's constant sacrifice. She comprehends the simple fact that George is a man, that he has reacted simply as a man to the beauty of the girl when he "took her over to the old Argyle gin and slept with her." She understands that it is with his possession and his knowledge of such facts, literally the facts of life, that he defends the Fairchilds *against* the intrusion of fact, against all that comes, like the train, bearing down upon them. She suspects, perhaps, that the Fairchild women are vaguely aware of the condescension in his nobility, aware that he can *afford* to indulge them in their disparagement and ignorance of fact, the fact of the outside world which begins at Memphis, simply because he does know it so well and because the knowledge is supremely self-suffcent. She suspects that it is out of chagrin at this element of his attitude, at their own half-realized envy of his knowledge, his knowledge of life present and real, that they continue to shade his glory under the image of the dead Denis. She knows that he has worked the device of disparagement on her, in telling her what he has done with the girl, protecting *her* from too sudden a vision of what beauty it is (not the garnet pin!) that is lost in the wood, that she has lost and the world knows; but she knows also that George's act has *not* degraded the girl's beauty, that if anything it has enhanced it. In short, she knows George—George the unknowable.

But beyond all of this even, beyond Ellen's or all the characters' conscious experience of it together, the legend serves as a unifying force. Ba-

sically, the train and the bridge (trestle) are communication symbols. In
Ellen's case, the relationships she discovers in the light of the incident result
in the one most nearly perfect personal communication of the story. The
separate incidents of the trestle episode itself and of her meeting with the
girl in the wood are brought together in her mind, after the photographer
has told the wedding party of the girl his train has killed on the way down
from Memphis, in a single, comprehensive vision which opens the way to
her wordless communication with George at the dance. But the most important significance of her experience in the whole purposes of the novel is
not for our interest in her, her effort to know George personally; her insight
is important, rather, simply as an example of the kind of structural relationships that are to be seen. We have to go on to see that the Yellow Dog
is also the train that has brought Laura to Shellmound—still another visitant
from the outside world, and a permanent one, since she is heiress to Marmion.
It brings even the shepherd crooks, ironically, and other furnishings for the
wedding, from Memphis. We have to see, further, that the symbols, characteristically, work both ways. That is, the legend for some means the failure
of communication—for Robbie with the family, as we have seen, and for
Shelley with Dabney, the engagement to Troy having closed a door upon
Shelley's understanding of her sister, perhaps even upon her sympathy with
the entire family.

Or, another way of putting it is that Ellen's "knowing" George is, after
all, only a final understanding of the fact of his independence, the fact that
he *is* unknowable. The legend makes George himself a symbol. Ellen spe-
cifically repudiates her "young girl's love of symbols" in her final attitude
toward George—that is, the sort of thing that the Fairchilds make of him.
Hers is a vision of the unmanageable *fact* of him. But Ellen's, perhaps, is a
schoolgirl's understanding of the term. And in the larger purposes of the
novel he remains a symbol; not entirely the Fairchilds' symbol—but his very
factuality itself becomes symbolic. It is notable that none of the *men* in the
novel admit the reader very often to their minds. Such is the Fairchild
women's notion of their men, which the author accepts as a technical principle, that they are a kind of serviceable gods—infinitely capable, having
access to wonderful powers of the outer world, and always *decently* keeping
their own counsel. And if one uneasily suspects, with Ellen, that George is
actually godlike in his manhood, that his stalwart impenetrability is not a
matter of decency, but of *having* some counsel to keep, an unsearchable
purpose—still this is only the excess of heroic typicality. As the reader has
to know him, as he functions in the novel, the legend has made him—with
the final qualification only that it has made all the Fairchilds too, and not,
as they sometimes suppose, they the legend. (This is the point, of course,

of Shelley's realization, when she runs the car across the tracks in front of the Yellow Dog, that it won't do to try "contriving" it.)

As an example of George's symbolic function, we may consider again Laura's experience. Ellen's, in fact, is not quite so exclusive an understanding of George as it might at first appear. At her childish level, Laura has entertained the same vision—of his necessary isolation, we will remember, and felt "matter-of-factly intimate" with the fact of the isolation, with him. And potentially this experience is a basis of sympathy between Laura and Ellen in the little girl's effort to make herself a part of the family. But George has "brought them together" without any conscious intention, without any rational understanding even of what is happening in the situation, either on his part or theirs. There is no willed, in the usual sense *personal* communication anywhere in the relationship. George functions here, then, precisely in the way that the various symbolic *objects* function to establish, and to illuminate, certain relationships. George is, in fact, the ultimate embodiment of the author's subtle conception of the subject-object relationship which is symbol—the object *informed* by, inseparable from, an always quickening, always manifest, but always inscrutable intelligence.

The people, then, as well as things, are carried out of themselves by the legend. And, finally, the significance of the particular story carries outside itself to other stories; every legend is all legend. The way in which we have seen the thread of the trestle incident becoming involved with Ellen's reflections upon the fate of the girl she met wandering in the woods—the girl and the meeting figure in the statement of what might be followed out as a distinct, major theme in itself, the theme of loss—is but one illustration of the complexity of the structure. The symbols of the trestle story are actually parts of certain larger, extended motives. The train is one of several means of transportation which have a symbolic function, more or less explicit, wherever they appear. The horses—Troy's horse, the horse which George gives to Dabney (having thought of it, significantly, when Robbie took his car to run away in), the horse which Dabney rides on her visit to her aunts (carrying a "wedding-present home on horseback"); the cars too—George's car which Robbie has wrecked, the new Pierce Arrow (all cars are still comparatively new), the darkened car which Dabney and Troy ride away in after the wedding, the lighted car in which the mayor and his family arrive for the reception. And so on. The trestle, over Dry Creek, is closely related to what may be loosely defined as the *water* motive—the bridge over the bayou "whose rackety rhythm Laura remembered," the old stories of the whirlpool, Laura's trip to Marmion with Roy when in a kind of baptismal ceremony she is pushed into the Yazoo and loses Ellen's garnet pin.

And any one of dozens of incidents, observations, unspoken perceptions, can become the "central" nexus in the whole complexity of interconnection. One need not start with the trestle episode or with any of the more obviously prominent incidents. One such observation as Shelley's at the reception— of the contrast between the darkened car of the newlyweds and the lighted car bringing the mayor, that "had come up alight like a *boat* in the night" (italics mine)—is enough. The simile has associations—we might assume at this level even somewhat consciously felt by Shelley—as remote as the comparison, early in the story, of a certain lamp in the living room at Shellmound to "a lighted shoe-box toy, a 'choo-choo boat' with its colored paper windows." Here, with the recollection of the dear and familiar object of their childhood play, the lamp itself having the radiance of its associations too already mingled with the light of the toy, is much of the pathos of Shelley's ironic realization that the public gaiety of the wedding party, the extraneous and trivial display of the "occasion" which the visit of so inconsequential and alien a personage as the mayor epitomizes, is a mockery of that darkness of marriage which has closed between her and Dabney. (The darkness which is the inevitable privacy of any marriage, the darkness which for Shelley is especially associated with Troy Flavin, of his hateful "overseer's soul," of the blood of Negroes on the floor of the office.) But beyond any possibility of Shelley's consciousness of the significance of her thought, the *boat* suggests all boats—the boat in which Laura rode with Roy when *she* saw Marmion, the house which is to be hers eventually, not Dabney's, and when she was admitted to the mystery of the Yazoo, the river that measures the time or the timelessness of the Fairchild world. (The prophesy of Shelley's fear for her sister's marriage is not, perhaps, altogether dark.) Or, reinforcing the first effect, the light, the lamp, is all the lamps—the heirloom night-light which Dabney broke.

One can follow a single object through the significance of its reappearances. The garnet pin—first as Battle's gift, and then through Ellen's use of her dream about it as a lullaby-story to Bluet, associated with her motherhood, the symbol both of loss and of gain; figuring in a re-statement of the same theme in her meeting with the girl in the wood; in her effort to get Partheny's assistance in finding it, becoming the symbol of the old Negress's second sight; appearing finally as the central symbol in an incident which embraces all these themes, the womb-return descent of Laura into the waters of the Yazoo. "As though Aunt Studney's sack had opened after all, like a whale's mouth, Laura opening her eyes head down saw its insides all around her—dark water and fearful fishes." And the pin, lost in the water, becomes the image of a relationship between Laura and her new mother Ellen, between her and the Fairchilds a union in the untold *secret* of the loss, which is more enduring even than what she had hoped for as a reward for her finding and returning the jewel.

One could, and would, go on. Devious ways are open from any point. But perhaps with this much of detail, we can hazard a few conclusive generalizations.

To return to the question of Miss Welty's attitude toward the society which she depicts, it should be apparent by now that in terms of approval or disapproval the evidence is mixed. In Ellen's vision of the hero, George, what appears to be a devastating criticism is implicit—the Fairchilds' "myth of happiness" would seem to be myth clearly in the worst sense, a childish retreat from reality. And it is possible to infer that the "wedding" of Dabney and Troy is a mockery of the failure of true marriage everywhere—even the marriage of Battle and Ellen; the marriage of the Fairchilds with the past, or with the future, whichever way one wants to approach it; the marriage of minds among all the characters.

But perhaps the crucial point of the problem is the status of the Negroes. If it must be admitted that Miss Welty does, as we have already suggested, "accept" the Fairchilds' typical attitude here—I think that acceptance is finally, though not perhaps quite so clearly, like her acceptance of the women's attitude toward the men. It is an acceptance as a technical principle only, and one which comes in at a deeper level for some very heavy qualification. For the purposes of that double attitude of pastoral which William Empson has defined, as well as in a more practical sense for people like the Fairchilds, the Negroes are a great convenience. It is at the expense of these "*rude* swains" that the Fairchilds can be the "*gentle* swains" (to use Milton's phrases for it) that they are—so that we can at once look down upon the narrow complacency, and envy the imaginative and moral richness, of their country simplicity. But Miss Welty implicitly recognizes the "convenience" for what it is. And the recognition is, in fact, very closely tied in with that problem of the women's attitude toward the men.

Dabney's preparation for her marriage are, significantly, associated with her riding forth into the fields. Troy Flavin emerges partially as a kind of "field god," similar to Floyd in *At the Landing*, or Cash in *Livvie*. And the mystery of his virility is in the present situation very closely connected, of course, with his intimate knowledge of the Negroes. It is this of which Shelley is at once so afraid and so contemptuous when she finds Troy settling a fight among the Negroes in the overseer's office. And the phrase of her reflection on her way back to the house, her wondering if "all *men*" are like him, makes the connection with George's role. George too, about whom Dabney is thinking on her ride to visit her aunts, is marked with the *blood* of the Negroes—he with the blood of compassion when he caught the knife and bound up the wounds of the little Negro boy, Troy with the blood of his knowledge of the Negroes in their labor. But, the significance of such distinctions as the latter aside, they are *men*—George coming naked from the water to catch the knife, Troy the dark figure on a horse that Dabney catches sight of on her way to her aunts' house; and their tolerence for the blood of Negroes is an essential part of their maleness. And Dabney senses something of this, the part that a new knowledge of the lives of the Negroes, of their intimacy with the earth, must play in the rebellion from her family which her marriage represents.

But this is the crucial point also in the sense that Dabney's discovery of the male mystery is clearly hopeful for the society as well as critical of it. Troy *is* the field god, and as such he is a principle of rejuvenation. The marriage promises ultimately, perhaps, not disruption but renewal, or renewal out of the disruption. And while Troy's is in a sense an influence from outside, it is defined, as we have seen, and complemented, partially by the role of George—and that, paradoxically, as an essential part of his status as the family hero. It can hardly be denied that Miss Welty does see the strength for rejuvenation as in part the family's own strength, the strength of their own myth as they themselves understand it, though she sees with equal clarity the limitations of that understanding.

Or, if the argument requires further elaboration, one must not forget that central to the old aunts' family sense is the *reverence* for disaster. Primrose insisted that people keep "their kinfolks and their tragedies straight." And there is reason to believe that they can accommodate Dabney's breaking the lamp too, that her breaking it is one with her keeping it ultimately, the "present" is given and must be kept whether she will or no, whether the "little old piece of glass" is kept intact or not. The themes of protection and disaster are inextricably bound up together from the first, in the family legend as in the design of the lamp and its shade, and their unity is unbreakable. Accepting the implicit pun on *present*—perhaps the marriage of past and present is not broken; perhaps that quality of the Fairchilds which is at first so baffling to Laura, their being so intensely "of the moment," is simply the result of their feeling supremely confident of their footing in the past. And, finally, Laura herself—who comes closer than anyone else to being Miss Welty's stand-in in the novel—remains to live with the family on terms which are, though again qualifiedly, both sympathetic and hopeful.

And yet I would insist that the question of approval or disapproval, of a prophesy of hope or disaster, is still not the key to Miss Welty's final attitude. Her principal interest in the society, her sympathy with it, is for the *vision* which it supports. We need not trouble ourselves ultimately over the fate of the society as such, or its worth in itself, or even the problem of whether it ever existed or could exist, actually, quite as it is pictured. The picture is *right* enough, in every sense, to provide the vision. And that is unquestionable—the novel itself, its living form, the constant order and quickness of its sensibility, is the essential proof of the vision. In fact, the novel *is* the vision. And I do not see, from the evidence of the novel itself, that Miss Welty is especially either disturbed or elated by the prospects of the actual Fairchild world. she is simply, like Laura with George, for the all-important moment "matter-of-factly intimate" with the dual paradox of the pastoral outlook—that all human society being ultimately suspect, the vision *must* to some extent condemn the society which produces it, and yet that the particular society which makes this truth most apparent is the "best" society.

This is the essential *realism* of Miss Welty's art. This is how her intensely narrow view—the concentration of her narrative which requires more than two hundred pages for the treatment of the events of a few days in the life of a hopelessly provincial family—becomes precisely at its most restricted a world-view.

But the last scene of the novel sums up the situation. We come back to the mind with which we began—Laura McRaven's mind. And Laura achieves her sense of "belonging" at last. She has been told that she is to stay, that Marmion is to be hers some day. The picnic, for her, is a celebration of her reception as a member of the family. But she accepts the decisions from the first with the secret thought that sometime she may go back to Jackson, to her father. The reservation does not diminish her present joy. But it is there. And the moment at which she feels most overwhelmingly at one with the family is when she can hardly see any of them, but sees *with* them the falling star. The "star" *is* a star—single, remote and inaccessibly, indifferent. and if it is not quite indifferent, if it does belong to the family in their common seeing, then it is *falling*. And yet, for the moment of its falling, it brings them together. Laura, and the Fairchilds, and the star, are one in the light of the star—and turning again with a gesture of embracing them, she embraces the firmament, "both arms held out to the radiant night." That one moment of pure vision, the people themselves in darkness, unseen, the star unseeing, becomes the sufficient thing in itself—the one thing.

RUTH M. VANDE KIEFT

The Mysteries of Eudora Welty

In explaining one of her own stories in "How I Write," [Eudora Welty] says, "Above all I had no wish to sound mystical, but I did expect to sound mysterious now and then, if I could: this was a circumstantial, realistic story in which the reality *was* mystery."

Miss Welty's stories are largely concerned with the mysteries of the inner life. She explains that to her the interior world is "endlessly new, mysterious, and alluring"; and "relationship *is* a pervading and changing mystery; it is not words that make it so in life, but words have to make it so in a story. Brutal or lovely, the mystery waits for people wherever they go, whatever extreme they run to." The term "mystery" has here to do with the enigma of man's being—his relation to the universe; what is secret, concealed, inviolable in any human being, resulting in distance or separation between human beings; the puzzles and difficulties we have about our own feelings, our meaning and our identity. Miss Welty's audacity is to probe these mysteries in the imaginative forms of her fiction. The critic's task is to try to follow her bold pursuit analytically and discursively, to state what the mysteries are, and to show how she tries to communicate them.

II

We begin with the story called "A Memory," which might be recognized as more or less autobiographical even if Katherine Anne Porter (in her sympathetic introduction to *A Curtain of Green*) had not suggested it first, because here in seminal form are some of the central mysteries which have occupied Eudora Welty as a mature writer. It is the *nature* of the child lying on the

From *Eudora Welty*. © 1962 by Twayne Publishers, Inc.

beach which suggests what is to come, her preoccupation and her discoveries. An incipient artist, the child has a passion for form, order, control, and a burning need to identify, categorize, and make judgments on whatever comes within her vision. She does this by making small frames with her fingers, which is her way of imposing or projecting order on a reality which she has already guessed but not admitted to be a terrifying chaos. She is convinced that reality is hidden and that to discover it requires perpetual vigilance, a patient and tireless scrutiny of the elusive gesture which will communicate a secret that may never be completely revealed.

Paralleled with this "intensity" is another equal intensity: that of her love for a small blond boy, a schoolmate about whom she knows nothing, to whom she has expressed nothing, but whom she holds fiercely within the protective focus of her love—a protection of him and of herself and her expectations which is enforced by the dreary regularity of school routine. But one day the boy suddenly has a nosebleed, a shock "unforeseen, but at the same time dreaded," and "recognized." It is the moment when she receives her first clear revelation of mortality, when she perceives the chaos that threatens all her carefully ordered universe, and the vulnerability of her loved one; she recognizes the sudden violence, the horror of reality, against which she is helpless. This event makes her even more fiercely anxious about the boy, for she "felt a mystery deeper than danger which hung about him."

This event is also a foreboding of the experience the girl has on the beach when a family-group of vulgar bathers comes crashing into the world of her dream. Here is wildness, chaos, abandonment of every description, a total loss of dignity, privateness, and identity. There is destruction of form in the way the bathers protrude from their costumes, in the "leglike confusion" of their sprawled postures, in their pudgy, flabby figures; there is terrifying violence in their abuse of each other, their pinches and kicks and "idiotic sounds," their hurdling leaps, the "thud and the fat impact of all their ugly bodies upon one another." There is a hint of a final threat to human existence itself when the man begins to pile sand on the woman's legs, which "lay prone one on the other like shadowed bulwarks, uneven and deserted," until there is a "teasing threat of oblivion." The girl finally feels "a peak of horror" when the woman turns out her bathing suit "so that the lumps of mashed and folded sand came emptying out . . . as though her breasts themselves had turned to sand, as though they were of no importance at all and she did not care." The girl has a premonition that without form— the kind she has been imposing on reality by her device of framing things like a picture—there is for human beings no dignity nor identity, that beyond the chaos of matter lies oblivion, total meaninglessness. This is the vision of reality which must be squared to the dream; and so the girl must now watch the boy, still vulnerable, "solitary and unprotected," with the hour on the beach accompanying her recovered dream and added to her love.

This is one of the sorrowful or "brutal" mysteries which Miss Welty presents in her stories. The "joyful" mystery is, of course, the careful, tender, ravishing love, the exquisite joy, and the dream. Chaotic reality does not displace the dream; though reality proves to be as terrifying as the child might have guessed, the dream cannot be totally destroyed.

The same mystery is explored in "A Curtain of Green," for the brooding, fearful, scarcely conscious anticipation of the girl in "A Memory" is the anguished knowledge of the bereaved young widow, Mrs. Larkin. In this story we have a similar careful, protective, absolute love, to which comes the violent affront of the most freakish and arbitrary kind of accident: a chinaberry tree simply falls on and kills Mrs. Larkin's husband. When she sees the accident, she assumes instinctively that the power of her love can save him: she orders softly, "You can't be hurt," as though, like God, she can bring order out of chaos. "She had waited there on the porch for a time afterward, not moving at all—in a sort of recollection—as if to reach under and bring out from obliteration her protective words and to try them once again . . . so as to change the whole happening. It was accident that was incredible, when her love for her husband was keeping him safe." Human love is finally powerless against chaos.

Now the young widow must penetrate deeply the meaning of this reality, which is simply to ask the question raised by any devastating accident: why did it happen? She plunges herself into the wild greenness out of which death fell: nature unpruned, uncultivated, formless in its fecundity. In the process of plunging, she hopes to discover the essential meaning of nature; the knowledge itself will give her a kind of power over it, even though paradoxically she must abandon herself to it, become a part of it, lose her identity in it, as she does with her hair streaming and tangled, her uncertain wanderings, her submersion in the "thick, irregular, sloping beds of plants." She must look to see what is concealed behind that curtain of green.

Into the focus of her attention comes Jamey, the Negro gardener, and once again she tries to seize control of destiny and effect her will, to give some meaning to the confusion and disorder of reality. If her love cannot preserve life, at least her fury and vengeance can bring death. Jamey's mindless serenity, his elusive self-possession, his quiet, inaccessible apartness (which signifies his calm acceptance of life) goad her into wonder and fury. For a moment she experiences a terrible lust for destruction. "Such a head she could strike off, intentionally, so deeply did she know, from the effect of a man's danger and death, its cause in oblivion; and so helpless was she, too helpless to defy the working of accident, of life and death, of unaccountability. . . . Life and death, she thought, gripping the heavy hoe, life and death, which now meant nothing to her but which she was compelled continually to wield with both her hands, ceaselessly asking, Was it not possible to compensate? to punish? to protest?" Out of oblivion—without malice or motive—she can cause a death, as her husband's death has come, motiveless, out of oblivion; yet her destructive action would also be meaningless because it is *not* compensation for her husband's death: it is even too pointless to be a protest; what would the protest be against? Life and death are arbitrarily given and taken, pointlessly interchangeable—how then can her action, or any human action, have meaning? And yet, how can a human being *not* protest?

No rational answer comes to Mrs. Larkin. There is only release, touched off by the sudden fall of a retarded rain: thus it is a chance of nature which saves her from committing a meaningless murder, just as it is a chance of nature which kills her husband. The rain seems to bring out the quiet and lovely essences, the inner shapes of things in all the profusion of that green place, for "everything appeared to gleam unreflecting from within itself in its quiet arcade of identity." Mrs. Larkin feels the rush of love ("tenderness tore and spun through her sagging body"); she thinks senselessly, "it has come" (the rain and the release). She drops the hoe, and sinks down among the plants in a half-sleep, half-faint, which is resignation; a blissful surrender to the mystery of nature, to the inevitable, because "against that which is inexhaustible, there was no defense." But her sleep has the look of death: there is the suggestion that ony by sinking herself into final oblivion will she ever be released from her burning compulsion to wrest meanings from nature, to impose order on chaos, to recover her loved one.

These dark mysteries are further explored in a story called "Flowers for Marjorie." The story takes place during the Depression, and Howard and Marjorie, a poor young Mississippi couple, have gone to New York City to find work. Marjorie is pregnant, and Howard has been engaged in a humiliating and fruitless search for a job. He has now reached a point of despair in which he imagines that nothing can ever happen to break the inevitability of the pattern of being without work, without food, without hope. In his view there is no slight possibility of change or chance, a stroke of good luck; time, like their cheap alarm clock, ticks on with a bland, maddening pointlessness, because for Howard time has stopped.

But Marjorie, a warm feminine girl with soft cut hair, quietly and literally embodies an assumption of the significance of time, change, and progression. She has the matter-of-fact, yet deeply mystical knowledge that her rounding body holds a new life. She looks forward to a birth, and to Howard she seems in a "world of sureness and fruitfulness and comfort, grown forever apart, safe and hopeful in pregnancy"—the one flagrant exception to the fixed pattern of hopeless and pointless repetition. As if to tease Howard with the knowledge of her enviable exemption from despair, she has by chance found a bright yellow pansy which she places in the buttonhole of her old sky-blue coat and looks at proudly—"as though she had displayed some power of the spirit." In her human hope and submission, her gentle and loving reproaches against Howard's anxiety, she seems to him almost "faithless and strange, allied to the other forces." He finally shouts at her, out of his deep love turned into terrible despair, "just because you can't go around forever with a baby inside your belly, and it will really happen that the baby is born—that doesn't mean everything else is going to happen and change! . . . You may not know it, but you're the only thing left in the world that hasn't stopped!"

Then in a moment of wild objection to the affront of time and change in her whole being, of her content, security, and easiness, he seizes a butcher knife and stabs her quickly and without violence—so quickly that the girl stays poised in a perfect balance in her seat at the window, one arm propped on the sill and hair blowing forward in the wind; the relative stillness and composure of her life now become the absolute, ironic stillness of death. Howard watches her lap like a bowl slowly filling with blood. Then he hears the clock ticking loudly, and throws it out the window. By his action he has taken a destructive hold of time and change, correcting the only apparent flaw in his desperate logic of futility.

The events which follow can only be described as monstrous. Howard, half-numb and hysterical, flings, himself on the town, only to be confronted with a series of crazily ironic pieces of good luck. It is as though chance had seized him by the throat and said, "You suppose nothing can happen to change the pattern, and *you* try to seize control. Oh, the universe is full of surprises—only *see* what can happen!"—and then throttled him and taken a gleeful revenge by playing a series of ingenious tricks on him. What a surprise when the small bright world of the glass-ball paperweight is deluged in a fury of snow, and when a man unaccountably drops a dime in his hand! What a surprise when the slot machine at the bar responds to his last last nickel by disgorging itself so profusely that one of the men says, "Fella, you ought not to let all hell loose that way" (for the crazy logic of hell *has* been let loose since Howard has committed the murder)! And what a finally horrifying surprise when he walks through a turnstile to an arcade and becomes "the ten millionth person to enter Radio City," covered with all of the honor and glory of arbitrarily conferred distinction and publicity ("What is your occupation?" "Are you married?"—as photo-lights flash) and given a huge key to the city and an armful of bright red roses!

He flees in terror back to the flat. There in the little fourth-story room, full of the deep waves of fragrance from the roses, he "knew for a fact that everything had stopped. It was just as he had feared, just as he had dreamed. He had had a dream to come true." Here he is with his gift of flowers for his lovely flower-loving wife (whose round and fruitful lap should be filled with roses instead of a pool of blood)—his good luck, his "break," his "dream come true." And here he is also with his nightmare come true. He now faces the impossibility of any personally significant kind of chance or change or hope, the absolute and unalterable fact of death.

If love and happiness seem to be permanently insured (as in Mrs. Larkin's case), chance may annihilate them at a stroke; if misery and destruction seem unalterable, so that from despair people act in accordance with what they suppose to be their tragic inevitability (as in Howard's case), chance may surprise them, belatedly and irrelevantly, with a shower of gifts. Human beings cannot predict, they cannot control, they cannot protest against, they cannot even begin to understand the inscrutable workings of the universe.

III

These are the darkest mysteries that Miss Welty ever explores, for in no other stories does she confront her characters with all the terrors of chance and oblivion. However inarticulate, plaintive, lonely, or frustrating she shows love becoming in the experience of a human being, she never again reveals it in its final and stark impotence against the implacable inhumanity of the universe. The stories tell us something about her philosophical vision, which might be identified (at the risk of giving her work the "tweak of fashion" she deplores) as pessimistic and existential.

Through the experience of her characters she seems to be saying that there is no final meaning to life beyond the human meanings; there is no divine "surround," no final shape to total reality, no love within or beyond the universe (for all its ravishing beauties), however much of it there may be burning in individual, isolated human hearts. Through an inevitable act of mind and heart (which is like a blessed reflex, because love comes willy-nilly, or a compulsion, because the mind must impose its order), the individual makes whatever meaning is to come out of chaotic reality, and this is the existential act. There are only fragments of shape and meaning, here, there, and everywhere: those created by all the world's lovers and artists (the terms often become interchangeable in her vocabulary). And in Miss Welty's catholic and charitable vision, the lovers and artists would probably include most people at least some of the time. Thus her deepest faith is couched securely in her deepest scepticism.

One other story in which she plunges into metaphysical questions is "A Still Moment." In this story three men try to wrest final meanings out of human life from three different points of view. Each of these men—Lorenzo Dow, the evangelist; Murrell, the outlaw; and Audubon, the naturalist—is consumed with a desire to know, or do, or communicate something of burning urgency; and each is essentially frustrated in his mission. Lorenzo, consumed by divine love, has the passion to save souls, but his efforts are mocked not only by lack of response—his inability to light up all the souls on earth—but by far more threatening internal struggles. These come from his awareness that nature mocks him in its simplicity, peace, and unconscious effectiveness; that he is more susceptible to nature than to divine beauty; and that in his frequent encounters with death he manages to survive less because of his sense of divine guidance and protection than because some strange savage strength and cunning overtake him in the moment of danger. He is saved by an instinct which he identifies as the word of the devil, not an angel, because "God would have protected him in His own way, less hurried, more divine." Because of his precarious and costly faith and the doubts and frustrations and waste places of his own heart, he flies across the wilderness floor from one camp meeting to the next, filled with the terrible urgency of his message: "Inhabitants of time! The wilderness is your souls on earth. . . . These wild places and these trails of awesome loneliness lie nowhere, nowhere but in your heart."

Murrell, the outlaw killer, who believes himself to be possessed of the devil, falls in beside Lorenzo and settles on him for his next victim. His method is strangely ceremonial, for he rides beside the victim telling long tales, in which a "silent man would have done a piece of evil . . . in a place of long ago, and it was all made for the revelation in the end that the silent man was Murrell himself, and the long story had happened yesterday, and the place *here*." Lorenzo's passion is to save the inhabitants of time before Eternity; Murrell's is to "Destroy the present! . . . the living moment and the man that lives in it must die before you can go on." In the moment of hideous confrontation with the victim just before the murder, Murrell tries to lay hold on the mystery of being. He murders for the same reason that Mrs. Larkin almost murders Jamey: "It was as if other men, all but himself, would lighten their hold on the secret, upon assault, and let it fly free at

death. In his violence he was only treating of enigma." Approaching the
point of climax which is to be the still moment, he and Lorenzo are like
brothers seeking light; for Lorenzo's divine passion is darkened by his sense
of the tempter within him, and Murrell is less guilty than his crimes would
make him appear because he has no other motive for killing than pure quest
for the elusive mystery of being. Evangelist and murderer, soul-saver and
destroyer, seem to become as one.

Audubon's light step on the wilderness floor, his serene and loving gaze
at the earth, and the birds and animals around him, suggest at first a sharp
contrast with the desperate urgency of the two men. He is a man who seems
in harmony with nature, "very sure and tender, as if the touch of all the
earth rubbed upon him"; a man who needs no speech because it is useless
in communicating with birds and animals. But Audubon is presently seen
to have his own urgency. The sweet excess of love gives him a compulsive
and insatiable need to remember, to record in his journal, and to convey all
the varieties of nature about him. His vigilant probing of nature is a quest
for origins and ends; he does not know whether the radiance he sees is only
"closed into an interval between two darks," or whether it can illuminate
the two darks which a human being cannot penetrate, and "discover at last,
though it cannot be spoken, what was thought hidden and lost." His endless
examination of the outside world may disclose to him the mystery of his
own identity. "When a man at last brought himself to face some mirror
surface he still saw the world looking back at him, and if he continued to
look, to look closer and closer, what then? The gaze that looks outward must
be trained without rest, to be indomitable."

Here gathered in the wilderness, then, are three fiery souls, each absolute
in its consuming desire, for "what each of them had wanted was simply *all*.
To save all souls, to destroy all men, to see and to record all life that filled
this world—all, all. . . ."

Into the still moment comes the beautiful, slow, spiral flight of the
snowy heron; with its unconscious freedom, it lays quiet over them, un-
burdens them, says to them, "Take my flight." To each comes a revelation
and these revelations are inevitably disparate and subjective. With swift joy
Lorenzo sees the bird as a visible manifestation of God's love. Murrell has
a sudden mounting desire for confession, and a response of pity; he wishes
for a keen look from the bird which could fill and gratify his heart: as though
the bird had some divine power, and its sign of recognition could accuse
and forgive simultaneously. Audubon gazes at the bird intensely as if to
memorize it; and then, because he knows he cannot paint accurately enough
from memory, he raises his gun to shoot it. As he does so, he sees in Lorenzo's

eyes horror so pure and final as to make him think he has never seen horror before.

Audubon shoots the bird and puts it in his bag. The three men disperse, and for each of them it is as though his destiny has been sealed, the basic issue of his life clarified. Murrell lies in wait for the next victim: "his faith was in innocence and his knowledge was of ruin; and had these things been shaken? Now, what could possibly be outside his grasp?" He is filled with his glorious satanic dreams of conquest and darkness.

Audubon knows that he will paint a likeness of the bird which will sometimes seem to him beautifully faithful to its original; but this knowledge comes with the tragic awareness that even though he alone as artist has really *seen* the bird, he cannot possess or even reproduce the vision because his painting will be a dead thing, "never the essence, only a sum of parts." The moment of beauty can never be communicated, "never be one with the beauty in any other man's head in the world. As he had seen the bird most purely at its moment of death, in some fatal way, in his care for looking outward, he saw his long labor most revealingly at the point where it met its limit." The final frustration of the artist is that he can never capture the final mystery of life, nor convey it to others; no matter how faithfully and sensitively reproduced, nature remains inviolable and unknown.

Riding slowly away, Lorenzo has a terrifying vision, for it suddenly seems to him that "God Himself, just now, thought of the Idea of Separateness." He sees no apparent order or scheme in the divine management of things, because God is outside Time, and He does not appear to know or care how much human beings who live inside Time need order and coherence which alone can bring the lover to a final union with the loved object. God created the yearnings, but He did not provide a way of meeting the need. He seems to Lorenzo finally indifferent:

> He could understand God's giving Separateness first and then giving Love to follow and heal in its wonder; but God had reversed this, and given Love first and then Separateness, as though it did not matter to Him which came first. Perhaps it was that God never counted the moments of Time; Lorenzo did that, among his tasks of love. Time did not occur to God. Therefore—did He even know of it? How to explain Time and Separateness back to God, Who had never thought of them, Who could let the whole world come to grief in a scattering moment?

In terms of the incident Lorenzo is saying: "Why did you let me see the bird, which was inevitably to love it, and see in it your love become visible, and share that love with the other watchers, only to let it be suddenly and pointlessly destroyed, so that I am now separated both from the beloved object, and from all who saw it or who might have seen and loved it?" Which is like saying, "Why do you allow death to happen?"—the question which also tortures the young wife in "A Curtain of Green."

Yet the "beautiful little vision" of the feeding bird stays with Lorenzo, a beauty "greater than he could account for," which makes him shout "Tempter!" as he whirls forward with the sweat of rapture pouring down his face. This is because he has again felt in his heart how overwhelmingly sensitive he is to the beauty of nature, and also how pointless and baffling is any attempt to relate it to divine love or meaning or plan or purpose; how pointless, then, is his mission to save souls. But he rushes on through the gathering darkness to deliver his message on the text "in that day when all hearts shall be disclosed." His final desperate gesture of faith is that when Time is over, meanings will be revealed; then the breach between Love and Separateness, the source of human tragedy, will be eternally closed. It is a faith that Miss Welty herself nowhere affirms: she only shows us, in the richly varied characters and situations of her stories, the intensity of the Love, and the tragic fact of the Separateness in the only life we know, which is our present life in Time. Miss Welty is asking metaphysical questions, but she is attempting no answers. The only solution to a mystery is yet another mystery; cosmic reality is a nest of Chinese boxes.

IV

With a sensitivity as detached as it is tender, so that we may not even notice the sympathy because of the sure, cool objectivity of her art (like Audubon, she is a careful and relentless observer), Miss Welty brings to life a number of characters each engaged in the private quest for the identity of the self, and the self in relation to the other. She is concerned about what she calls "the mystery of relationship" in all stages of awareness. The questions asked are "Who am I and who are you?" These are related to the questions "How can I get my love out into the world, into reality"—that is, communicated and understood—and "How can I see and know what is going on in *your* heart," which is sometimes to say, "How can I see my love returned and shared?"

In "The Hitch-Hikers" and "Death of a Traveling Salesman," two salesmen have a flash of insight into their own identity, which is pathetically and paradoxically that they *have* no identity because they have no place and no focus of love to define them. Tom Harris, the thirty-year-old salesman of

"The Hitch-Hikers," appears to have been born with a premonition of his coming isolation, for as a child he had often had the sense of "standing still, with nothing to touch him, feeling tall and having the world come all at once into its round shape underfoot and rush and turn through space and make his stand very precarious and lonely." He lives in a world of hitch-hikers, and the title suggests that Harris himself is one of the transients despite the relative economic security provided by his job.

Tom Harris is a wise, tolerant, generous sort; people naturally confide in him and women are attracted to him, but he will not be held back by anyone. He is beyond surprise or shock because of his wide experience. With a peculiarly detached kind of suspense he views the events surrounding a murder committed in his car by one of the hitch-hikers, and this is because any strong emotion or violence in his life has always been something encountered, personally removed. There had been "other fights, not quite so pointless, but fights in his car; fights, unheralded confessions, sudden love-making—none of any of this his, not his to keep, but belonging to the people of these towns as he passed through, coming out of their rooted pasts and their mock rambles, coming out of their time. He himself had no time. He was free; helpless." Without an ounce of exhilaration in the knowledge of his freedom, and embracing with apparent resignation his knowledge of helplessness, he is found in the last scene poised for yet another flight, a puzzling, touching American phenomenon, exceptional only in the degree of his self-awareness.

The salesman of "Death of a Traveling Salesman," R. J. Bowman, comes to this awareness belatedly, by perceiving with the acute eye of a stranger the essence of the simple, rooted life of the couple whose crude hospitality he briefly enjoys. The painful contrast with his own loveless, rootless ways kills him as much as does the protest of his troublesome heart. By the end of the story he is beautifully ready for love, but he cannot live to enjoy it. The best comment on the two salesman stories is Miss Welty's own in quite another context—her essay on the importance of place in fiction: "Being on the move is no substitute for feeling. Nothing is. And no love or insight can be at work in a shifting and never-defined position, where eye, mind, and heart have never willingly focused on a steadying point." Just *seeing* this truth is enough to kill a man, although his salvation may lie in having seen it.

The salesmen barely got started in their quest for love and identity; but Clytie, in the story by that name, though less self-aware, has made some small progress. She is ready to emerge, to reach out toward others: she is full of the wonder and mystery of humanity, and there is a kind of breathless, religious awe in the way she scans the faces of the townspeople, seeing the absolute and inscrutable uniqueness of each one. "The most profound, the most moving sight in the whole world must be a face. Was it possible to comprehend the eyes and the mouths of other people, which concealed she knew not what, and secretly asked for still another unknown thing? . . . It was purely for a resemblance to a vision that she examined the secret, mysterious, unrepeated faces she met in the street of Farr's Gin." To the people of Farr's Gin, Clytie is ready to give that most generous of all gifts— contemplation: the desire to know without using, the respect for "otherness," the awe of what is inviolable. But she is suffocated and nauseated, living in a house of disease and death with her vampire-like sister, her alcoholic brother, her apoplectic father, and the dead brother with a bullet hole in his head. These faces come pushing between her and the face she is looking for, which is a face that had long ago looked back at her once when she was young, in a sort of arbor: "hadn't she laughed, leaned forward . . . and that vision of a face—which was a little like all the other faces . . . and yet different . . . this face had been very close to hers, almost familiar, almost accessible."

After a horrible experience in which, with "breath-taking gentleness," she touches the face of a barber who comes to shave her father, only to find it hideously scratchy, with "dense, popping green eyes," she dashes out to the old rain barrel, which seems to her now like a friend, and full of a wonderful dark fragrance. As she looks in, she sees a face—the face she has been looking for—but horribly changed, ugly, contracted, full of the signs of waiting and suffering. There is a moment of sick recognition, "as though the poor, half-remembered vision had finally betrayed her." That knowledge compels her to do the only thing she can think of to do: she bends her head down over and into the barrel, under the water, "through its glittering surface into the kind, featureless depth, and held it there."

What does her action mean? First of all, that she sees the ghastly dis-parity between what she once was and ought to have been (the loving, laughing creature of her youth) and what she has become (ugly, warped, inverted). Also, perhaps, she realizes that the only love in that house, if not in that town, was the love *she* made: there was no one then to embrace, no nature to plunge into but her own, no love possible but narcissistic love, no reality but her own reality, no knowledge possible but the knowledge of death, which is the immersion into oblivion. It is another pointless joke in a pointless universe. The final image of her as fallen forward into the barrel, "with her poor ladylike black-stockinged legs up-ended and hung apart like a pair of tongs," is one of the most grim jokes Miss Welty has ever perpetrated: it is only our memory of the wild misfiring of Clytie's love which makes us hear the narrator say, "See her coldly as grotesque, but see her also tenderly as pathetic."

The situations in all these stories seem fundamentally tragic or pathetic. It is when the loving heart is awakened in finding an object that joy speaks out in the stories, almost inaudibly in "First Love," somewhat more clearly in "At the Landing," and loudly and triumphantly in "A Worn Path." Joel Mayes, the solitary little deaf-mute of "First Love," is dazzled into love by a single gesture of Aaron Burr's, a gesture which brings a revelation:

> One of the two men lifted his right arm—a tense, yet gentle and easy motion—and made the dark wet cloak fall back. To Joel it was like the first movement he had ever seen, as if the world had been up to that night inanimate. It was like a signal to open some heavy gate or paddock, and it did open to his complete astonishment upon a panorama in his own head, about which he knew first of all that he would never be able to speak—it was nothing but brightness.

A single beautiful movement of human strength and careless grace has crystallized a love which is fated to be as inarticulate as it is sweetly wondering and intense. Quietly, night after night, the little boy sits watching his beloved, adoring his nobility, his mystery, his urgency. The boy's presence is accepted by the conspirators, but ignored. Joel has no way of expressing his love, except by trotting like a little dog around his master, sniffing out the dangers that lie in his path, for Joel constantly senses the imminence of disaster, and the dread of coming separation. "Why would the heart break so at absence? Joel knew it was because nothing had been told." And yet even if the moment of revelation *did* come, when love might speak out, he knows there are no words for what it might say. Gazing deeply into the face of the sleeping Burr, he has a terrible wish to speak out loud; "but he would have to find names for the places of the heart and the times for its shadowy and tragic events, and they seemed of great magnitude, heroic and terrible and splendid, like the legends of the mind. But for lack of a way to tell how much was known, the boundaries would lie between him and the others, all the others, until he died." The most he can do for Burr is to quiet his nightfears by gently taking his hand, stopping his nightmare ravings from the ears of potential eavesdroppers. When Burr leaves town Joel feels he will "never know now the true course, or the outcome of any dream." His love never gets *in the world*, but it is less pathetic than Clytie's because at least it has found an object, it has flowered.

"In the world" is a key phrase in the story of Jenny Lockhart called "At the Landing." It is the hearts of her family that are locked: she is caught in the house of pride, tradition, "culture," and death, folded in the womb of that house by her grandfather. Through the painful birth process of discovery

and experience she comes to the landing, the taking-off place, and so out
into the world. The world, the forces of life, are symbolized by the river
and the flood, which inundate. Jenny's house and the graveyard where her
relatives are buried. Billy Floyd, a wild creature of mysterious origins who
fishes on the river, rides along on the flood and is master of it, is the one
who brings her into the world: not only by his sexual violation of her, but
more quietly and surely through her adoring response to his wild beauty,
through the revelations which come to her about herself and him, and about
love, which are the chief concern of the story.

    Jenny learns almost as much about love, about its mysteries and changes,
and the mystery of human identity, as it is possible to learn. These revelations
come to her by seeing, feeling, and guessing—by intuitive perception. For
example, simply in watching Billy's innocence as he drinks deeply and then
throws himself on the grass to sleep, she knows her innocence has left her:
this is because a knowledge of innocence presupposes some knowledge of
experience, of what might *not* be innocent, out of which contrast springs the
recognition of innocence. Or she learns how love "would have a different
story in the world if it could lose the moral knowledge of a mystery that is
in the other heart": that is, if people who love were less aware of how both
vulnerable and inviolable their lovers were, they could speak their minds
more fully, ride over each other more freely with their aggressions, or attack
each other more analytically; but they could not, of course, learn much more
about each other, or achieve more satisfaction by doing so (even though,
human nature being what it is, they inevitably *will* do so). Watching Billy
ride the red horse becomes for her a kind of anticipation of the sexual act,
through which she learns that "the vaunting [male] and prostration [female]
of love told her nothing": that is, sexual experience in itself cannot disclose
the mystery of human identity nor bring people together.

    When she sees Billy Floyd in the village store, he seems changed: there
is "something close, gathering-close, and used and worldly about him, . . .
something handled, . . . strong as an odor, the odor of the old playing cards
that the old men of The Landing shuffled every day over their table in the
street." If she presses him now, corners him in that small place, she will
discover his identity, and that will be something small, mean, and faintly
dirty—for he is thought by the literal-minded to be "really the bastard of
one of the old checker-players, that had been let grow up away in the woods
till he got big enough to come back and make trouble." But he conquers her
with his defiant look, and she wisely lets him escape, knowing that this is
not his true and final definition: his origins are more wild and wonderful (is
the Natchez Indian in his blood?—is he one of the people of the lost Atlantis?);

his nature cannot be defined by the context of the village store and the odors of old playing cards.

She learns too the value of her love ("what my heart holds this minute is better than what you offer the least bit less"), and how enormously precious is her whole nature, which must be learned slowly, patiently, tenderly ("She looked outward with the sense of rightful space and time within her, which must be traversed before she could be known at all"). She knows also that "what she would reveal in the end was not herself, but the way of the traveler": that is, she has no final revelations to give to any lover; she is only herself, like every other human being, on a perplexing journey through life, engaged in the perpetual and difficult process of finding herself, her meaning, her destination. The most two people can do is to travel together for a while. Billy Floyd has his own search, and she has hers. These are only a few of the amazing discoveries Jenny makes in her birth process, the process of coming into the world; and each discovery is, of course, only the revelation of yet another human mystery. At the end of the story she is only starting her wait for Billy Floyd. She has "arrived," she has been born (and with what violence in that series of rapes at the hands of the river men); but she hasn't yet really begun the journey; she is "at the landing."

Jenny's love barely manages to get articulated; its actions in the world are fumbling and largely ineffectual; and at the end of the story she is left, like Joel, separated from her loved one. But the love of old Phoenix in "A Worn Path" is most triumphantly realized "in the world." It has a clear object—her grandson; it is actualized, put out into reality, not only by her care of him, but in the periodic ceremonial act of her trip along the worn path into town to fetch the "soothing medicine." There are no significant barriers to the expressive love of old Phoenix, and this is reflected also in her sense of familiarity with nature—the ease with which she talks to the birds and animals—and in her ability to live as readily, interchangeably, and effectively in the realm of the fanciful and supernatural as she does in the realm of practicalities. She is, like Dilsey in *The Sound and the Fury*, a completely and beautifully harmonious person—something one does not often find in the fiction of either Miss Welty or Faulkner.

V

What happens when love finds fulfillment in the most natural and happy way possible, physicaly and emotionally, when it is both communicated and returned and is solidly "in the world" socially and legally through marriage? Is there then an end to the mysteries of the self and the other? In several of her stories Miss Welty shows there is not; she indicated, in fact, that the one thing any married person cannot do is to assume knowledge of the other, or try to force it in any way, or make a predictable pattern of a relationship, or block the independence, or impede the search of the other. A relationship of love can be kept joyful, active, free, only if each partner steps back now and then to see the other with a fresh sense of his inviolable otherness, his mystery, his absolutely sacred and always changing identity. Out of some deep need to establish the new perspective, to insist on freedom and apartness, one partner may simply run away from the other, withdraw, or go into temporary "retreat." This is a basic situation in "A Piece of News," "The Key," "The Wide Net," *The Robber Bridegroom*, *Delta Wedding*, "Music from Spain," "The Whole World Knows," and "The Bride of the Innisfallen." The quarrels and separations presented in these stories are not the ordinary distressing marital quarrels which spring from hate, aggression, and conventional domestic discord, for none of these lovers has ceased to love or want the other. Each of them is simply demanding in his own way: "See me *new*. Understand the changes in me, and see how I am apart from you, unknowable and not to be possessed: only when you see me new can you possess me fully again."

The theme is given a semi-comic treatment in "A Piece of News." Ruby Fischer, a primitive, isolated and apparently unfaithful young backwoods wife, chances on a newspaper story in which a girl with the same name is shot in the leg by her husband. Though Ruby knows such an action on her husband Clyde's part to be quite improbable—even though he knows of her infidelities—she is immediately struck with the imaginative possibilities of such a situation, and is marvelously impressed and flattered. Images of herself dying beautifully in a brand-new nightgown, with a remorseful Clyde hovering over her, play delightfully in her mind. The romantic view of herself extends to her whole body; and while preparing dinner after Clyde returns, she moves in a "mysteriously sweet . . . delicate and vulnerable manner, as though her breasts gave her pain." When she discloses to Clyde the secret of the newspaper story, there is a moment, before common sense triumphs, when the two of them face each other "as though with a double shame and a double pleasure." The deed *might* have been done: "Rare and wavering, some possibility stood timidly like a stranger between them and made them hang their heads." For an instant they have had a vision of each other in alien fantasy roles—an experience which is pleasing, exciting, and rather frightening.

The theme is again treated with tender humor in "The Key." Ellie and Albert Morgan are dramatically shut off from the outside world by being deaf-mutes. When the story opens, we find them sitting tautly in a railroad station, waiting for the departure of their train to Niagara Falls. Ellie, a large woman with a face "as pink and crowded as an old-fashioned rose," is by far the stronger of the two. Little Albert, "too shy for this world," seems to be Ellie's own "homemade" product, as though she had "self-consciously knitted or somehow contrived a husband when she sat alone at night." But he is neither defeated nor submissive: there is an occasional sly look in his eye which tells of a secret hope and anticipation, a waiting for some nameless surprise indefinitely withheld.

It comes at last in the form of a key accidentally dropped by a young man, a curious red-haired stranger who bears some kinship to Harris of "The Hitch-Hikers" and to George Fairchild of *Delta Wedding*. He is marvelously fiery, young and strong, compassionate, sensitive, with a lovingly humorous detachment. But the observer-narrator senses that he will "never express whatever might be the desire of his life . . . in making an intuitive present or sacrifice, or in any way of action at all—not because there was too much in the world demanding his strength, but because he was too deeply aware." His life is both full of giving and empty of permanent commitment; he has Harris' freely floating love and weariness.

The key, which drops apparently out of the sky at Albert's feet, immediately becomes the thing he has been waiting for, richly portentous—he sits there glowing with "almost incandescent delight." The young man senses this and doesn't reclaim the key; he stands apart watching the fingers go as Albert and Ellie talk in their own private language. What does it mean? Maybe now they'll really fall in love at Niagara Falls; maybe they didn't have to marry just because they were afflicted and lonely; maybe they can love, be happy, like other people. They wait importantly and expectantly.

But they miss their train—they can't, of course, hear it coming and going so quickly. Shock! At once Ellie resumes her old mode of domination and organizes her "counter-plot" against the outside world, which is obviously hostile to their hopes and plans. But Albert refuses to be crushed now—he has the key; he is delightedly, securely inward. Ellie is baffled: she can't get through to him. Because the strange, funny, and pitiful little irony of their relationship is that Ellie "talks" too much. When they are on the farm together and she feels some unhappiness between them, she has to break off from her churning to assure Albert of her love and protection, "talking with the spotted sour milk dripping from her fingers." All her talk just makes the fluid, simple, natural farm life "turn sour." Security runs away in the face of Ellie's panic.

Ellie sits there, heavy with disappointment as she thinks about Niagara

Falls, and her conviction that they would even *hear* it in their bodies through the vibrations. She is going to brood over the whole incident and the terrible disappointment, as she does over all their discussions, misunderstandings, agreements—"even about the secret and proper separation that lies between a man and a woman, the thing that makes them what they are in themselves, their secret life, their memory of the past, their childhood, their dreams. This to Ellie was unhappiness." She is afraid of Albert's private life, of all his secrets that cannot be hers. Loneliness and isolation compel her to claim *all*—to work herself into every corner of his pitifully limited experience. But Albert really isn't tamed despite his obedience—he stubbornly preserves his quiet, intensely personal identity, and he has the key to it in his pocket. Maybe the key wasn't, as he first thought, the symbol of a coming happiness through the Niagara Falls expedition; maybe it was "something which he could have alone, for only himself, in peace, something strange and unlooked for which would come to him." Poor Ellie.

But the red-haired stranger with his god-like compassion and omniscience (how much of all this does he guess?—the narrator seems to have infinite faith in his awareness), has a key for Ellie too. She is not to be left, literally or figuratively, out in the cold. The key he places in her hand bears the legend, "Star Hotel, Room 2." What could be neater or lovelier? The designated use to its owner of Albert's key is never disclosed. The imagination can soar on that one; it is appropriate as the symbol of Albert's secret hope, his own unique humanity, a thing shared with, endowed by the mysterious, god-like young man. Ellie's key to the young man's hotel room is appropriately practical—she is the one who "manages"; and yet it has its exciting edge. Why do honeymooners travel to Niagara Falls, after all, except to repair to hotel rooms? This room is in the *Star*, and that's what Ellie has been wishing on. Perhaps she will yet see her wish fulfilled for a "changing and mixing of their lives together."

But the story ends with the young man's faintly dismal, realistic vision, not of the possibilities, but of the probabilities. As he departs, lighting a cigarette, we can see his eyes by the light of the match, and in them, "all at once wild and searching, there was certainly, besides the simple compassion in his regard, a look both restless and weary, very much used to the comic. You could see that he despised and saw the uselessness of the thing he had done." He may have god-like prescience and compassion, but he hasn't the omnipotence—he can't *change* things.

Ellie and Albert are extraordinary, but their problem is not. People do not have to be deaf-mutes to be driven together by the felt hostility of the outside world, and the inevitable pattern then is one of a too insistent closeness. Ellie has to learn that Albert has a right to his secret—he'll keep that key in his pocket as long as he lives.

A version of this theme which bears some resemblance to the Cupid and Psyche myth appears in Miss Welty's romping fantasy, *The Robber Bridegroom*. Rosamond, the lovely heroine, has been kidnapped by a bold bandit of the forest; but she finds the arrangement much to her liking. The one prohibition—the forbidden fruit in her Eden—is any attempt to discover her bridegroom's identity, which is disguised by wild berry stain. Rosamond's idyllic state continues until the satanic stepmother tempts her to break the prohibition and provides her with a recipe for a brew to remove the berry stain. In the night when her bandit lover is sleeping, Rosamond wipes the stains off his face. He awakens, and she is distressed to find that he is only Jamie Lockhart, the well-scrubbed, dull, respectable young man who had come at the request of her father, Clement, to search for and capture the robber bridegroom. Jamie, in turn, now recognizes Rosamond as "Clement Musgrove's silly daughter," and both of them are thoroughly disenchanted with each other. The truth, as old Clement has seen even with his upside-down version of his daughter's predicament, is that "all things are double, and this should keep us from taking liberties with the outside world, and acting too quickly to finish things off." Once human mystery and complexity are ignored or dissipated by a pressing for simple definitions, the residue is bound to be disappointing.

A "lovers' quarrel" is the cause of the falling out between William Wallace and his newly pregnant, young wife Hazel in "The Wide Net." Hazel is filled with her great experience of coming motherhood: she is elated, solemn, fearful, mysterious, "touchy." Willam Wallace hasn't taken sufficient account of this: in fact, to make matters worse, he has been out on a drinking spree with one of the boys. Hazel retaliates by writing a letter in which she threatens to drown herself, And so her husband must now go in quest of her, and find, swimming in the depths of the Pearl River, what is the "old trouble":

> So far down and all alone, had he found Hazel? Had he suspected down there, like some secret, the real, the true trouble that Hazel had fallen into, about which words in a letter could not speak . . . how (who knew?) she had been filled to the brim with that elation that they all remembered, like their own secret, the elation that comes of great hopes and changes, sometimes simply of the harvest time, that comes with a little course of its own like a tune to run in the head, and there was nothing she could do about

it—they knew—and so it had turned into this? It could be nothing but the old trouble that William Wallace was finding out, reaching and turning in the gloom of such depths.

Though "The Bride of the Innisfallen" has been widely misunderstood, the real subject of that story is related to that of "The Wide Net." The point of view of most of "The Bride of the Innisfallen" is that of an observing narrator who obviously enjoys the human comedy in the train compartment full of richly varied "types" heading for Ireland, but it is a perspective subtly shared with that of one character singled out for special attention: a young American wife who is running away from her husband. Only at the end of the story does the narrator concentrate explicitly on the mind and experience of the young wife, but then we realize how what she has seen on the trip, and on her perambulations through glorious, fresh, wildly funny, dazzlingly lovely Cork (so it registers for her), *explain* both to us and to her what her "trouble" has been with her husband.

The "trouble" is her excess of hope, joy, and wonder at the mystery and glory of human life, all of which is symbolized to her in the lovely young bride who appears mysteriously on board the "Innisfallen" just as it prepares to land at Cork. This joy the American girl's husband apparently cannot see or share (as William Wallace cannot at first perceive Hazel's strange elation). "You hope for too much," her husband has said to her: that was "always her trouble." How can she preserve this quality which is so much and simply her definition that without it she loses her identity? The question answers itself, because joy and hope constantly bound up in her. "Love with the joy being drawn out of it like anything else that aches—that was loneliness; not this. *I* was nearly destroyed, she thought, and again was threatened with a light head, a rush of laughter. . . ." Her real problem is not how to preserve her joy, but how to communicate it to her husband, or to anybody:

> If she could never tell her husband her secret, perhaps she would
> never tell it at all. You must never betray pure joy—the kind you
> were born and began with—either by hiding it or by parading it
> in front of people's eyes; they didn't want to be shown it. And
> still you must tell it. Is there no way? she thought—for here I
> am, this far. I see Cork's streets take off from the waterside and
> rise lifting their houses and towers like note above note on a page
> of music, with arpeggios running over it of green and galleries
> and belvederes, and the bright sun raining at the top. Out of the
> joy I hide for fear it is promiscuous, I may walk forever at the
> fall of evening by the river, and find this river street by the red

rock, this first, last house, that's perhaps a boarding house now, standing full-face to the tide, and look up to that window—that upper window, from which the mystery will never go. The curtains dyed so many times over are still pulled back and the window looks out open to the evening, the river, the hills, and the sea.

There is no "reconciliation scene" in this story as there is in "The Wide Net." The girl leaves the story wandering off happily into a bar. From it she hears a cry flung out "fresh . . . like the signal for a song," and she walks into "the lovely room full of strangers"—people in whom she can delight without fear of exposure ("So strangeness gently steels us," Miss Welty has quoted a poem of Richard Wilbur). We do not know whether her husband will see her "new" when she returns to him, though we rather hope he may; for how can she possibly be resisted, this heavy-hearted little saint spinning so giddily toward heaven?

In a story called "Circe" (also from the volume titled *The Bride of the Innisfallen*), Miss Welty celebrates the human mystery by adopting the perspective of a superhuman being. The effort is a *tour de force*, because in her attempts to fathom the nature of Odysseus after she seduces him, Circe begins to look very much like one of Miss Welty's human lovers, more than one of whom gaze at the beloved when he is asleep, hoping at that unguarded moment to catch the elusive mystery of his identity. But as a sorceress and magician, though preserved from human frailty and tragedy, and all the uncertainties of time and circumstance (because she can predict the future), Circe envies the human condition. She first contrasts the way of her father with that of the earthly hero. Nature, here personified and deified, is seen to be inviably constant and serene, sure and effective, exempt from human pain, "suffering . . . no heroic fear of corruption through his constant shedding of light, needing no story, no retinue to vouch for where he has been." But in Circe's vision human beings have an equal, though different, glory. She thinks enviously,

> I know they keep something from me, asleep and awake. There exists a mortal mystery, that, if I knew where it was, I could crush like an island grape. Only frailty, it seems, can divine it—and I was not endowed with that property. They live by frailty! By the moment! I tell myself that it is only a mystery, and mystery is only uncertainty. (There is no mystery in magic! Men are swine: let it be said, and no sooner said than done.) Yet mortals alone can divine where it lies in each other, can find it and prick it in all its peril, with an instrument made of air. I swear that

only to possess that one, trifling secret, I would willingly turn
myself into a harmless dove for the rest of eternity!

For what is the "instrument of air"—a metaphor? Possibly imagination,
intuition, sensitivity, contemplation, wonder, love (whatever, one might
guess, is the opposite of cold, rational, loveless, destructive analysis—the
metaphor for which would be a blunt mechanical instrument). These delicate
"instruments" are the means by which human beings can probe the human
mystery, the means by which any lover may meet or be united with any
object in the world.

VI

It is also with these "instruments of air" that Miss Welty approaches
the persons and places and themes of her fiction; it is what makes for the
distinctively lyrical quality of her style. "Relationship is a pervading and
changing mystery," she says in "How I Write"; "it is not words that make
it so in life, but words have to make it so in a story." Her problem as an
artist has been to find the words to convey the mysteries, the elusive and
subtle inner states of mind and feeling for which most people (and certainly
the people of her fiction) have no words at all: she must be articulate about
what cannot be articulated. She is out on a fringe, lonely place—as lonely
as the wilderness in "A Still Moment"; there, like Lorenzo, Murrell, and
Audubon, she must press for definitions: the meanings, the names of some
of the most complex, elusive, and important of all human experiences. And
it is inevitable that she should have her failures as well as her successes. Her
language is not always adequate to the difficulty of what must be conveyed,
which is perhaps the reason why she has often been accused of being coy,
arch, perversely subtle, too nuanceful or precious.

The wonder is, after all, the large measure of her success. The reason
for this we may trace as far back as to the habit of the child in "A Memory,"
the habit of close observation, of recording, identifying, "placing" things; or
we may see it as recently expounded as in the small volume mentioned
earlier, *Place in Fiction*. "Place in fiction," Miss Welty says, "is the named,
identified, concrete, exact and exacting, and therefore credible, gathering-
spot of all that has been felt, is about to be experienced, in the novel's
progress." As she defines it, place is not only the region or setting of a story;
it stands for everything in a story that fixes it to the known, recognizable,
present, and "real" world of everyday human experience. It is like the solid

flesh that both encloses (pins down) and discloses (reveals) the more elusive human thoughts and feelings. "In real life," she says, "we have to express the things plainest and closest to our minds by the clumsy word and the half-finished gesture. . . . It is our describable outside that defines us, willy-nilly, to others, that may save us, or destroy us, in the world; it may be our shield against chaos, our mask against exposure; but whatever it is, the move we make in the place we live has to signify our intent and feelings." In fiction this illusion of reality is created if the author has seen to "believability": "The world of experience must be at every step, through every moment, within reach as the world of appearance." The inner world and the outer surface of life must be interrelated and fused; the imaginative vision must glow through the carefully, objectively painted exterior world.

In her best stories Miss Welty has seen to "believability" by her use of the familiar local Mississippi settings; her close descriptions of the appearance, manner, gestures of her characters; her infallible ear for their speech rhythms and idioms; her use of plausible and logical plot structures; her concern with physical texture and psychological validity; her use of proper names which are always solidly realistic, local, devastatingly accurate, and at the same time, often richly allusive in their symbolism. The destination of the salesman in "Death of a Traveling Salesman," for example, is a town called Beulah. Surprisingly enough, there *is* such a place: population 342, Boliver County, N.W. Mississippi, according to the *Columbia Gazetteer*; but the higher validity of its use as a place name is that the salesman is on his way to the "Beulah Land" of the Southern Baptist gospel hymns.

Or her concern with "believability" may be shown again in the way "A Still Moment"—as formally patterned a story and as close to allegory as any she has written—is most solidly wedded to history in place and time. For the wilderness is not only the isolated, mythical desert setting appropriate to mystical revelations, but it is the old familiar Natchez Trace many years back in history; the characters are not simply abstract or apocryphal types of missionary prophet (the good man), criminal (the evil man), and naturalist (the artistic, detached, contemplative man), but they are three historical persons about whom Miss Welty has undoubtedly done her piece of "research."

Most of all, the style itself is the best illustration of her concern with "believability." The fusion of the elusive, insubstantial, mysterious, with what is solidly "real," can be seen in almost any passage selected at random from Miss Welty's fiction. The one chosen is a short and relatively simple description from "The Death of a Traveling Salesman." In this episode

Sonny, the husband, has returned from a neighbor's with a burning stick in tongs; Bowman, the salesman, watches the wife lighting the fire and beginning preparations for supper:

> "We'll make a fire now," the woman said, taking the brand.
>
> When that was done she lit the lamp. It showed its dark and light. The whole room turned golden-yellow like some sort of flower, and the walls smelled of it and seemed to tremble with the quiet rush of the fire and the waving of the burning lampwick in its funnel of light.
>
> The woman moved among the iron pots. With the tongs she dropped hot coals on top of the iron lids. They made a set of soft vibrations, like the sound of a bell far away.
>
> She looked up and over at Bowman, but he could not answer. He was trembling.

In this passage the simple actions, sights and sounds, are conveyed to us sharply and precisely and yet mysteriously and evocatively, through the mind of a man who experiences an unconscious heightening of awareness, a clarity of vision, because in these closing hours of his life he is approaching his moment of revelation. He is feeling more deeply than ever before, and hence everything he sees he also feels intensely. We know that throughout the story he is in a semi-delirious state, and thus in realistic terms, we are prepared for all the adumbrations and overtones, the exaggerations, blurs, and distortions of his perception. But strange and elusive meanings are coming to him through all he sees: each act and gesture becomes almost ceremonial; each sight and sound richly allusive, portentous, beautiful, and deeply disturbing. The lamplight registers to him as both dark and light, suggesting the states of dream and reality, his feeling of the warmth, welcome and shelter of this home and his fear of being left out, as well as the chills and fever of his illness. His sense impressions are blended as the golden light seems to him like a flower with an odor that pervades the walls; the trembling, rushing, and waving of the light are also extended to include the walls, suggesting the instability and delirium of his impressions. The woman does not simply "walk" or "step": she "moves among" the iron pots, like some priestess engaged in a mysterious ritual, moving among the sacred objects; the sound of the hot coals dropped on the iron lids is muted, softly vibrating; the comparison to the sound of a bell again suggests the ceremonial resonance these simple actions have for the salesman. It is no wonder that at the end of the passage we find him trembling and speechless. Through the evocation of the language we have felt into his complex emotional state of wonder, fear, longing, sickness, pain, love: we have seen it all through his eyes and experience. This is characteristically the way Miss Welty blends the inner world and outer surfaces of life—the way she sees to "believability."

In observing and recording the mysteries, Miss Welty creates a response of wonder, terror, pity, or delight. Her stories teach us nothing directly except, through *her* vision, how to observe, and wonder, and love, and see the mysteries; for brutal or lovely, they wait for us wherever we go.

JOYCE CAROL OATES

The Art of Eudora Welty

W hat shocks us about this art is its delicate blending of the casual and
the tragic, the essential femininity of the narration and the subject, the reality,
which is narrated. How can the conversational and slightly arch tone of her
fiction give way to such amazing revelations? That horror may evolve out
of gentility—and, even in stories dealing with the very poor or the very
unenlightened, Miss Welty is always "genteel"—is something we are not
prepared to accept. Our natural instinct is to insist that horror be emphasized,
underlined, somehow exaggerated so that we may absorb it in a way satis-
fying to our sensibilities. Fiction about crime and criminals suggests always
the supreme importance of crime and criminals; it is a statement of moral
value. The kind of black comic-naturalism that has descended from Celine
also insists, heavily, upon a moral point, about the crazy depravity of the
world and the endless combinations and permutations in which it may be
located . . . and this too, though it is constructed as a kind of joke or a series
of jokes, may be related to a sense of proportion, a feeling that outrages
certainly deserve more attention than normal events.

Eudora Welty baffles our expectations. Like Kafka, with whom she
shares a number of traits, she presents the distortions of life in the context
of ordinary, even chatty life; she frightens us. I have no doubt that her
intentions are not to frighten anyone, or to make particular judgments on
life, but the effect of her fiction is indeed frightening. It is the bizarre
combination of a seemingly boundless admiration for feminine nonsense—
family life, food, relatives, conversations, eccentric old people—and a sharp,
penetrating eye for the seams of this world, through which a murderous

From *Shenandoah* 20 (Spring 1969), © 1969 by Joyce Carol Oates and Washington
and Lee University.

light shines. Flannery O'Conner, who was certainly indebted to Miss Welty's stories, abandons entirely the apparatus of "realism"; she has no patience for, no interest in, real people. Amazing as some of Flannery O'Connor's stories are, they are ultimately powerless to move us seriously—like the beautiful plays of Yeats, they are populated with beings not quite human. Eudora Welty's people are always human.

The most impatient and unsympathetic of readers will find himself drawn in gradually, even charmed, by the Fairchild clan of *Delta Wedding*. They are indeed a "capricious and charming Southern family" (quote from paperback edition cover). That the foundation of their charm, the leisure in which to develop their charm, is something wholly ugly and unacceptable— the obvious exploitation of Negroes, inside an accidental economic structure in which the Fairchilds are, certainly, American nobility in spite of their lack of real wealth—is something one comes to accept, just the same as one comes to accept the utter worthlessness of certain characters of James and Proust, in social and human terms, but maintains an interest in their affairs. And then it is stunning to realize, as one nears the conclusion of *Delta Wedding*, that in spite of the lovingly detailed story, in spite of her seemingly insatiable generosity toward these unexceptional people, Miss Welty understands clearly their relationship with the rest of the world. So much cute nonsense about a wedding!—and then the photographer announces, making conversation, that he has also taken a picture of a girl recently hit by a train. "Ladies, she was flung off in the blackberry bushes," he says; and Aunt Tempe says what every aunt will say, "Change the subject." The dead girl may have been as pretty and flighty and exasperating as the young bride, but her human value is considerably less. She is on the outside; she is excluded from society. Her existence is of no particular concern to anyone. So, a member of this claustrophobic and settled world may well venture into hers, make love to her, leave her, and her death is a kind of natural consequence of her being excluded from the "delta wedding" and all its bustling excitement. It is more disturbing for the mother of all those children to be told, by her Negro servant, that he quite seriously wishes all the roses were out of the world—"If I had my way, wouldn't be a rose in de world. Catch your shirt and stick you and prick you and grab you. Got thorns." Ellen trembles at this remark "as at some imprudence." Protected by her social position, her family, her condition of being loved, protected by the very existence of the Negro servant who must brave the thorns for her, it is only imprudence of one kind or another that she must tremble at.

In "The Demonstrators"—the O. Henry First Prize story of 1968—the lonely consciousness of an ordinary, good man is seen in a context of greater,

more violent loneliness, the terrible general failure of mankind. The demonstrators themselves, the civil rights agitators, do not appear in the story
and need not appear; their intrusion into the supposedly placid racist society
of this small Southern town is only symbolic. They too are not to be trusted,
idealistic as they sound. Another set of demonstrators—demonstrating our
human powerlessness as we disintegrate into violence—are the Negroes of
the town, a choral and anonymous group with a victim at their theatrical
center, one of themselves and yet a curious distance from them, in her death
agony.

The story begins with the semi-colloquial "Near eleven o'clock" and
concerns itself at first with the forceful, colorful personality of an aged
woman, Miss Marcia Pope. Subject to seizures as she is, crotchety and wise
in the stereotyped manner of such old dying ladies, she is nevertheless the
only person in town "quite able to take care of herself," as the doctor thinks
at the conclusion of the story; a great deal has happened between the first
and last paragraphs. The doctor's mission is to save a young Negro woman,
who has been stabbed by her lover with an ice pick; his attempt is hopeless,
the woman is bleeding internally, too much time has been wasted. And so
she dies. The doctor goes home and we learn that he himself is living a kind
of death, since his wife has left him; his wife left him because their thirteen-
year-old daughter, an idiot, had died. . . . everything is linked to everything
else, one person to another, one failure to another, earlier, equally irreme-
diable failure. The doctor is "so increasingly tired, so sick and even bored
with the bitterness, intractability that divided everybody and everything."
The tragedy of life is our permanence of self, of Ego: but this is also our
hope, in Miss Welty's phrase our "assault of hope," throwing us back into
life.

The next morning he reads of the deaths of the Negro lovers, who
managed to kill each other. The homespun newspaper article concludes, "No
cause was cited for the fracas." The doctor had not failed to save the Negro
woman and man because there was never the possibility of their being saved.
There was never the possibility of his daughter growing up. Of the strange
failure of his marriage nothing much is said, yet it too seems irreparable.
But, as he looks into the garden, he distinguishes between those flowers
which are "done for" and those which are still "bright as toys." And two
birds pick in the devastation of leaves, apparently permanent residents of
the garden, "probing and feeding."

"The Demonstrators" resists analysis. It is a small masterpiece of subtlety, of gentleness—a real gentleness of tone, a reluctance to exaggerate or
even to highlight drama, as if sensing such gestures alien to life. We are left

with an unforgettable sense of the permanence and the impermanence of life, and especially of the confused web of human relationships that constitute most of our lives. The mother of the dying Negro girl warns her, "*I* ain't going to raise him," speaking of the girl's baby. Of course she is going to raise him. There is no question about it. But the warning itself, spoken in that room of unfocussed horror, is horrible; the grotesque has been assimilated deftly into the ordinary, the natural.

It is an outstanding characteristic of Miss Welty's genius that she can write a story that seems to me, in a way, about "nothing"—Flaubert's ideal, a masterpiece of style—and make it mean very nearly everything.

REYNOLDS PRICE

The Onlooker, Smiling: An Early
Reading of The Optimist's Daughter

On March 15, this year *The New Yorker* published an issue half filled with
a story by Eudora Welty called *The Optimist's Daughter*. The story is some
30,000 words long, 100 pages of a book—much the longest work published
by Miss Welty in fourteen years, since her fourth collection of stories, *The
Bride of the Innisfallen* in 1955. In those years, in fact, fewer than twenty
pages of new fiction by her have appeared (two extraordinary pieces rising
from the early civil rights movement, "Where Is the Voice Coming From?"
and "The Demonstrators"). Now there is this novella—and, close behind it,
news of a long comic novel, more stories, a collection of essays.

A *return*, in our eyes at least (Miss Welty could well ask "From where?");
and some eyes (those that haven't raced off after the genius-of-the-week) have
got a little jittery with time. Returns in the arts are notorious for danger—
almost always stiff-jointed, throaty, short-winded, rattled by nerves and
ghosts of the pressures which caused the absence. There have been rare and
triumphant exceptions—among performers in recent memory, Flagstad and
Horowitz, grander than ever. But who among creators? American arts are
uniquely famous for silent but audibly breathing remains—novelists, poets,
playwrights, composers. The game of naming them is easy and cruel, and
the diagnoses multiply. Yet why must I think back seventy years to Verdi's
return with *Otello* thirteen years after *Aïda* and the Requiem for an ample
precedent to Miss Welty's present achievement?

I have known the new story for less than a month and am straining
backward to avoid the sort of instant apotheosis which afflicts the national
book-press; but I don't feel suspended over any fool's precipice in saying
this much—*The Optimist's Daughter* is Eudora Welty's strongest, richest work.

From *Shenandoah* 20 (Spring 1969). © 1969 by Washington and Lee University.

For me, that is tantamount to saying that no one alive in America now has yet shown stronger, richer, more useful fiction. All through my three readings, I've thought of Turgenev, Tolstoy, Chekhov—*First Love*, *The Cossacks*, *The Steppe*—and not as masters or originals but as peers for breadth and depth.

And an effortless power of *summary*, unity (of vision and means). For that is what I have felt most strongly in the story—that Miss Welty has now forged into one instrument strands (themes, stances, voices, genres) all present and mastered in various pieces of earlier work (many of them, invented there) but previously separate and rather rigidly compartmented. I'm thinking especially of "comedy" and "tragedy." In her early work—till 1955— she tended to separate them as firmly as a Greek dramatist. There is some tentative mingling in the larger works, *Delta Wedding* and the linked stories of *The Golden Apples*; but by far the greater number of the early stories divide cleanly—into rural comedy or farce, pathos or tragic lament, romance or lyric celebration, lethal satire. This is not to say that those stories overselect to the point of falsification (fear and hate lurk in much of the laughter, laughter in the pain); but that the selection of components-for-the-story which her eye quickly or slowly made and the subsequent intensity of scrutiny of those components (place, character, gesture, speech) exhibited a temporary single-mindedness as classical as Horace's, Vermeer's.

But now in *The Optimist's Daughter* all changes. If the early work is classic, this might be medieval—in its fullness of vision, depth of field, range of ear. Jesus *and* goblins, Macbeth *and* the porter. There is no sense however of straining for wholeness, of a will to "ripeness," no visible girding for a major attempt. The richness and new unity of the story—its quality of summary—is the natural image produced by *this action* as it passes before Miss Welty's (literal) vision—look at a room from the perfect point, you can see it all. She has found the point, the place to stand to see this story—and we discover at the end that she's seen far more than that. Or perhaps the point drew her—helpless, willing—towards it, her natural pole?

For it is in this story that she sustains most intensely or has the fullest results extracted from her by the stance and line-of-sight which, since her first story, have been native to her—that of the onlooker (and the onlooker's avatars—the wanderer, the outsider, the traveling salesman, the solitary artist, the bachelor or spinster, the childless bride). Robert Penn Warren in his essay "Love and Separateness in Eudora Welty" defined the stance and theme as it formed her early stories—

> We can observe that the nature of the isolation may be different
> from case to case, but the fact of isolation, whatever its nature,

provides the basic situation of Miss Welty's fiction. The drama which develops from this basic situation is of either of two kinds: first, the attempt of the isolated person to escape into the world; or second, the discovery by the isolated person, or by the reader, of the nature of the predicament.

And a catalogue of her strongest early work and its characters is a list of onlookers, from R. J. Bowman in "Death of a Traveling Salesman" (her first story) and Tom Harris in "The Hitch-Hikers" (both lonely bachelors yearning for the richness which they think they glimpse in the lives of others—mutual love, willful vulnerability), to the young girl (a would-be painter) in "A Memory" and Audubon in "A Still Moment" (the artist who must hole-up from life, even kill it, to begin his effort at description and comprehension), to the frightening and hilarious spinsters of "Why I Live at the P.O." and *The Ponder Heart* or the more silent but equally excluded Virgie Rainey of *The Golden Apples*, to the recently orphaned Laura who visits her Fairchild cousins in *Delta Wedding* as they plunge and surface gladly in their bath of proximity, dependence, love.

You might say—thousands have—that the onlooker (as outsider) is the central character of modern fiction, certainly of Southern fiction for all its obsession with family, and that Miss Welty's early stories then are hardly news, her theme and vision hardly unique, hardly "necessary," just lovely over-stock. Dead-wrong, you'd be.

In the first place, her early onlookers are almost never freaks as they have so famously been in much Southern (and now Jewish) fiction and drama. (Flannery O'Connor, when questioned on the prevalence of freaks in Southern fiction, is reported to have said, "It's because Southerners know a freak when they see one.") They have mostly been "mainstream" men and women—in appearance, speech and action at least. Their visions and experiences have been far more nearly diurnal—experiences comprehensible at least to most men—than those of the characters of her two strong contemporaries, Carson McCullers and Flannery O'Connor, whose outsiders (often physical and psychic freaks) seem wrung, wrenched, from life by a famished special vision.

In the second place, the conclusions of Miss Welty's early onlookers, their deductions from looking—however individual and shaped by character, however muted in summary and statement—are unique. Their cry (with few exceptions, her salesman the most eloquent) is not the all but universal "O, lost! Make me a *member*" but something like this—"I am here alone, they are there together; I see them clearly. I do not know why and I am not happy but I *do* see, and clearly. I may even understand—why I'm here, they there. Do I need or want to join them?" Such a response—and it is, in Miss Welty, always a response to vision, literal eye-sight; she has the keenest eyesight in American letters—is as strange as it is unique. Are we—onlookers to the onlookers—moved to sympathy, acceptance, consolation? Are we chilled or appalled and, if so, do we retreat into the common position?— "These people and their views are maimed, self-serving, alone because they deserve to be. Why don't they have the grace to writhe?" For our peace of mind (the satisfied reader's), there is disturbingly little writhing, only an occasional moment of solemn panic—

> "She's goin' to have a baby," said Sonny, popping a bite into his mouth.
>
> Bowman could not speak. He was shocked with knowing what was really in this house. A marriage, a fruitful marriage. That simple thing. Anyone could have had that.
>
> Somehow he felt unable to be indignant or protest, although some sort of joke had certainly been played upon him. There was nothing remote or mysterious here—only something private. The only secret was the ancient communication between two people. But the memory of the woman's waiting silently by the cold hearth, of the man's stubborn journey a mile away to get fire, and how they finally brought out their food and drink and filled the room proudly with all they had to show, was suddenly too clear and too enormous within him for response . . .

Or a thrust through the screen, like Lorenzo Dow's in "A Still Moment"—

> He could understand God's giving Separateness first and then giving Love to follow and heal in its wonder; but God had reversed this, and given Love first and then Separateness, as though it did not matter to Him which came first. Perhaps it was that God never counted the moments of Time . . . did He even know of it? How to explain Time and Separateness back to God, Who had never thought of them, Who could let the whole world come to grief in a scattering moment?

But such moments are always followed by calm—Bowman's muffled death or Dow's ride onward, beneath the new moon.

Yet in those early stories the last note is almost invariably rising, a question; the final look in the onlooker's eyes is of puzzlement—"Anyone could have had that. Should I have tried?" Not in *The Optimist's Daughter* however. The end clarifies. Mystery dissolves before patient watching—the unbroken stare of Laurel McKelva Hand, the woman at its center. The story is told in third person, but it is essentially seen and told by Laurel herself. At the end, we have not watched a scene or heard a word more than Laurel; there is not even a comment on Laurel which she, in her native modesty, could not have made aloud. That kind of secret first-person technique is at least as old as Julius Caesar and has had heavy work in modern fiction, where it has so often pretended to serve Caesar's own apparent aim (judicial modesty, "distancing") while in fact becoming chiefly a bullet-proof shield for tender egos, an excuse for not confronting personal failure (Joyce's *Portrait* is the grand example), a technical act of mercy. But Laurel Hand is finally merciless—to her dead parents, friends, enemies, herself; worst, to us.

This is what I understand to be the story—the action and Laurel's vision of the action.

Laurel Hand has come on sudden notice (and intuition of crisis) from Chicago, where she works as a fabric designer, to a New Orleans clinic where her father Judge McKelva, age 71, is being examined for eye trouble. (The central metaphor begins at once—vision, the forms of blindness; the story is as troubled by eyes as *King Lear*; and our first exposure to Laurel's sensibility suggests youth and quivering attentiveness.) In a clinic she has time to notice this—

> Dr. Courtland folded his big country hands with the fingers that had always looked, to Laurel, as if their simple touch on the crystal of a watch would convey through their skin exactly what time it was.

Laurel's father is accompanied by his new wife Fay; and at the diagnosis of detached retina, Fay's colors unfurl—hard, vulgar, self-absorbed, envious of Laurel and, in Laurel's eyes, beneath the McKelvas's and Laurel's dead mother. The doctor advises immediate surgery, over Fay's protests that nothing is wrong. The judge declares himself "an optimist," agrees to eye-repair; the surgery goes well, and Laurel and Fay take a room in New Orleans to spell one another at the Judge's bedside—their important duty, to keep him still, absolutely motionless with both eyes bandaged through days of recovery. Friction grows between the two women but with no real discharge. Fay shows herself a kind of pet, baby-doll—her idea of nursing consisting of descriptions of her new shoes or earrings, her petulance at missing Mardi Gras whose time approaches loudly through the city. Laurel watches quietly, reading Dickens to her father, oppressed by his age and docility—

> He opened his mouth and swallowed what she offered him with the obedience of an old man—obedience! She felt ashamed to let him act out the part in front of her.

Three weeks pass, the doctor claims encouragement, but the Judge's deep-ening silence and submission begin to unnerve Fay and to baffle Laurel. (It is only now—nearly fifteen pages in—that we learn Laurel's age. She is older than Fay and perhaps Fay is forty. We are, I think, surprised. We had felt her to be younger—I'd have said twenty-four and only now do I notice that she bears a married name; yet no husband has been mentioned and will not be till just before the midpoint of the story. There is no air of caprice or trick about these crucial withholdings, only quiet announcement—"Now's the time for this.") Then on the last night of Carnival, Laurel in her rooming house senses trouble and returns to the hospital by cab through packed, raucous streets. (Inevitably, a great deal of heavy holy weather will be made over Miss Welty's choice of Carnival season for this opening section and the eve of Ash Wednesday for the first climax. So far as I can see, she herself makes almost nothing of it—the revelry is barely mentioned and then only as a ludicrously inappropriate backdrop to death. Even less is made of the city itself, almost no appeal to its famous atmosphere—it is simply the place where a man from the deep South finds the best doctors.) At the hospital, Laurel finds her fore-knowledge confirmed. Fay's patience has collapsed. She shakes the silent Judge, shouts "Enough is enough"; and Laurel enters to watch her father die—

> He made what seemed to her a response at last, yet a mysterious response. His whole pillowless head went dusky, as if he laid it under the surface of dark pouring water and held it there.

While Laurel and Fay await the doctor's confirmation in the hospital lobby, they watch and listen to a Mississippi country family come to oversee their own father's death—the Dalzells, family of the Judge's deranged roommate. (Their sizable appearance is not, as might first seem, a chance for Miss Welty to ease tension and pass necessary clock-time with one of her miraculously observed country groups. Funny and touching as they are—

> "If they don't give your dad no water by next time round, tell you what, we'll go in there all together and pour it down him," promised the old mother. "If he's going to die, I don't want him to die wanting water"—

the Dalzells make a serious contribution towards developing a major concern of the story. They are, for all their coarse jostling proximity, a *family* of finer feeling and natural grace than whatever is constituted here by Fay and Laurel; and they will soon return to mind, in sweet comparison with Fay's Texas kin who swarm for the funeral.) At final news of the Judge's death, Fay lunges again into hateful hysterics; but Laurel tightens—no tears, few words. Only in the ride through revellers toward the hotel does Laurel begin to see, with a new and steelier vision, meanings hung round people, which she does not yet speak—

> Laurel heard a band playing, and another band moving in on top of it. She heard the crowd noise, the unmistakable sound of hundreds, of hundreds of thousands, of people *blundering*.

Part II opens with the train ride home to Mount Salus, Mississippi. (Laurel's view from the train of a single swamp beech-tree still keeping dead leaves begins to prepare us for her coming strangeness, her as yet unexpected accessibility to ghosts.) Mount Salus is a small lowland town and is now home only to the dead Judge—Fay will inherit Laurel's childhood home but is Texan forever; Laurel will return to Chicago soon. But two groups of her friends survive in the town—her dead parents' contemporaries and her own schoolmates—and they rally to her, ambivalent hurtful allies, as Fay's kin—the Chisoms—arrive for the funeral. Led by Fay's mother, they cram the Judge's house like a troupe of dwarfs from a Goya etching, scraping rawly together in a dense loveless, shamingly vital, hilarious parody of blood-love and loyalty—"Nothing like kin. Yes, me and my brood believes in clustering just as close as we can get." It is they—Fay's mother—who at last extract from Laurel what we have not yet known, that Laurel is a widow—

> "Six weeks after she married him . . . The war. Body never recovered."
> "*You* was *cheated*," Mrs. Chisom pronounced . . . "So you ain't got father, mother, brother, sister, husband, chick nor child." Mrs. Chisom dropped Laurel's finger to poke her in the side as if to shame her. "Not a soul to call on, that's you."

So the Chisoms stand at once—or pullulate—in Laurel's sight, as a vision of the family and of love itself as horror, hurtful, willfully vulnerable, parasitic. Yet one of them—Wendell, age seven, viewing the corpse—also provides her with a still point for temporary sanity, for "understanding" Fay and her father's love for Fay—

> He was like a young, undriven, unfalsifying, unvindictive Fay. His face was transparent—he was beautiful. So Fay might have appeared to her aging father, with his slipping eyesight.

That emergency perception and the cushioning care of friends prop Laurel through Fay's last hysterical kiss of the corpse and on through the burial.

—Propped but stunned, and open on all sides—especially the eyes—for gathering menace to her saving distance. Above the graveyard, she sees a flight of starlings—

> black wings moved and thudded in perfect unison, and a flock of migrant starlings flew up as they might have from a plowed field, still shaped like the grounds of the cemetery, like its map, and wrinkled in the air.

And afterwards, at the house again, she numbly accepts more insults from Fay and waits out the slow departure of the Chisoms—taking Fay with them for a rest in Texas.

Part III is the longest of the four parts, both the story's journey through the underworld and the messenger of what the story learns there. It has four clear divisions. In the first, Laurel entertains four elderly ladies, friends of her parents, who raise a question so far unasked (among the signs of mastery in the story, one of the surest is the patience, the undefended gravity with which Miss Welty answers—or asks—all the reader's questions in her own time not his, and finally makes him admit her justice). The question is, why did Judge McKelva Marry Fay?—"What happened to his judgment?" One of the ladies flatly states that Laurel's to blame; she should never have married but stayed home and tended her widowed father. Laurel makes no defense, barely speaks at all till the same lady weakens and begins "forgiving" Fay—

> "Although I guess when people don't *have* anything . . . Live so *poorly*—"
> "That hasn't a thing to do with it," Laurel said.

This new ruthlessness (a specific defeat of her own attempt to forgive Fay through the child Wendell) calms in the following scene—Laurel alone in her father's library. Here, because of a photograph, she thinks for the only time in our presence of her own marriage—"Her marriage had been of magical ease, of *ease*—of brevity and conclusion, and all belonging to Chicago and not here." But in the third scene—Laurel's contemporaries, her brides-maids, at drinks—she bristles again, this time to defend her parents against affectionate joking—"Since when have you all thought my father and mother were just figures to make a good story?" Her friends retreat, claim "We weren't laughing at them. They weren't funny." (Laurel accepts the clari-fication; only at the end, if faced again with "They weren't funny" might she offer correction, huge amplification.) The fourth scene is longest, strang-est, the crisis—from which Laurel, the story, all Miss Welty's earlier on-lookers and surely most readers emerge shaken, cleared, altered. On her last

night in Mount Salus before returning to Chicago and before Fay's return,
Laurel comes home from dinner with friends to find a bird flying loose
indoors, a chimney sweep. She is seized at once by an old fear of birds (we
are not reminded till the following morning that a bird in the house means
bad luck ahead), and in panic shuts herself into her parents' bedroom—now
Fay's—against its flight. Here alone and silent except for sounds of wind
and rain, among her parents' relics, she endures her vision—of their life,
hers, the world's. Her initial step is to calm herself, to examine the sources
of her recent angers, her present terror—

> What am I in danger of, she wondered, her heart pounding. Am
> I not safe from *myself*?
>   Even if you have kept silent for the sake of the dead, you cannot
> rest in your silence, as the dead rest. She listened to the wind,
> the rain, the blundering, frantic bird, and wanted to cry out, as
> the nurse cried out to her, "Abuse! Abuse!"

What she first defines as the "facts" are these—that her helpless father had
been assailed and killed by his own senseless, self-absorbed young wife and
that she—his only child—was powerless to save him but can now at least
protect his memory. Protect—and flush her own bitterness—by exacting
justice from Fay, extracting from Fay an admission of her guilt. Yet Laurel
knows at once that Fay, challenged, would only be baffled, sealed in genuine
blind innocence. Balked in advance then by invincible ignorance, is Laurel
to be paralyzed in permanent bitterness? She can be, she thinks, released
and consoled by at last telling someone—the facts, the names. But tell whom?
Her own mother, long since dead. To tell her mother though—should that
ever be possible—would be an abuse more terrible than Fay's. Laurel can
only go on telling herself and thereby through her perpetual judging become
a new culprit, another more knowing Fay. That is—and can go on being—
"the horror." At that moment, desperate with rage and forced silence, she
makes the only physical movement open (the bird still has her trapped in
the room). She retreats into an adjoining small room. It had been her own
nursery, where she'd slept near her parents; then the sewing room; now a
closet where Fay has hidden Laurel's mother's desk. Here, memory begins—
a long monologue (yet always in third person) which bears Laurel back
through her parents' lives, her life with them. (The structure and method
of these fifteen pages at first seem loose, old-fashioned. No attempt is made
through syntax or ellipsis to mimic the voice or speed of Laurel's mind, to
convince us that we literally overhear her thoughts. Yet the process of memory proceeds with such ferocious emotional logic to an end so far beyond

Laurel's imagined needs or desires—Laurel's and ours—that we are at last convinced, as shaken as she.) The memories begin warmly—here are things they touched, relics of their love, a family desk, a small stone boat carved with her father's initials, his letters to her mother (which Laurel will not read, even now), a photograph of them in full unthreatened youth. In the flood of affection, Laurel begins to move from her old stance of onlooker to a conviction of having shared her parents' lives, been a corner of their love. She continues backward through memories of summers in the West Virginia mountains with her mother's family. (Both her parents' families were originally Virginian; and it would be possible—therefore someone will do it—to construct a kind of snob-machine with these genealogies: Virginians are finer than Mississippians are finer than Texans. The story says no such thing; only "This is what happened"—Miss Welty's own mother was from West Virginia, her father from Ohio.) Those summers, recalled, seem made of two strands—her mother's laughing immersion in family love and her own childish bafflement: tell me how much and why they love you, your mother and brothers. This early bafflement is focused for Laurel in her first sight of her grandmother's pigeons. Without claiming a mechanical connection which Miss Welty clearly does not intend, it is worth noting that this sight is the beginning (so far as we know) of Laurel's present personal distance, her stunned passivity in the face of the Chisoms feeding on one another—

> Laurel had kept the pigeons under eye in their pigeon house and had already seen a pair of them sticking their beaks down each other's throats, gagging each other, eating out of each other's craws, swallowing down all over again what had been swallowed before: They were taking turns . . . They convinced her that they could not escape each other and could not be escaped from. So when the pigeons flew down, she tried to position herself behind her grandmother's stiff dark skirt, but her grandmother said again, "They're just hungry, like we are."

It was a knowledge and revulsion which her mother had seemed to lack—until her long final illness at least. The terms of that illness are not fully explained—Laurel's mother went blind, lay in bed for years, growing slowly more reckless and condemnatory, more keensighted in her observation of husband and daughter as they hovered beside her helpless. As the illness had extended through five years (just after Laurel's widowhood) and as Laurel now recalls it, her mother had at last endured the awful knowledge in its simple killing progression—that we feed on others till they fail us, through their understandable inability to spare us pain and death but, worse, through the exhaustion of loyalty, courage, memory. In the pit of her illness, Laurel's mother had said to the Judge standing by her—

> "Why did I marry a coward?" . . . Later still, she began to say— and her voice never weakened, never harshened; it was her spirit speaking in the wrong words—"All you do is hurt me. I wish I might know what it is I've done. Why is it necessary to punish me like this and not tell me why?"

Then she had sunk silent toward her death, with only one last message to Laurel—"You could have saved your mother's life. But you stood by and wouldn't intervene. I despair for you." In the teeth of such judgment, Laurel's father—the optimist—had married Fay; had chosen to submit again to need, and been killed for his weakness. What had been betrayed—what her mother like a drugged prophetess had seen and condemned before the event—was not his first love but his first wife's *knowledge*, the dignity and achievement of her unanswerable vision. Fay's the answer to nothing. Then can love be?—Answer to what? Death and your own final lack of attention doom you to disloyalty. You're killed for your cowardice. With that news, the scene ends. Laurel sleeps.

> A flood of feeling descended on Laurel. She let the papers slide from her hand and put her head down on the open lid of the desk and wept in grief for love and for the dead.

—Grief surely *that* love had not saved but harrowed her parents, a love she had not shared and now can never.

Part IV is a quick hard but by no means perfunctory coda. Laurel wakes in early light, having slept at her mother's desk. Now unafraid, she leaves her parents' room, sees the exhausted bird perched on a curtain. Mr. Deedy, the blundering handyman, calls by to peddle spring chores. Laurel asks him in to catch the bird. He declares it bad luck and scares it around from room to room but only succeeds in making a nosey tour of the house. Then Missouri, the maid, arrives and she and Laurel gingerly arrange the bird's escape in the only passage of the story where the touch seems to me to press a little heavily, uneasily—

> "It's a perfectly clear way out. Why won't it just fly free of its own accord?"
>   "They just ain't got no sense like we have . . . All birds got to fly, even them no-count dirty ones . . ."

Laurel burns her mother's papers, saving only the snapshots and the carved stone boat. She calls herself a thief—the house and contents are Fay's now—but she justifies herself—

> It was one of her ways to live—storing up to remember, putting aside to forget, then to find again—hiding and finding. Laurel thought it a modest game that people could play by themselves, and, of course, when that's too easy, against themselves. It was a game for the bereaved, and there wasn't much end to it.

Her calm seems complete, her departure foregone and unprotested; but in a final look through kitchen cupboards, she finds her mother's breadboard—its worn polished surface inexplicably gouged, scored and grimy. Her numb peace vanishes, her rejection of revenge. She knows that, in some way, this is Fay's work, Fay's ultimate murder of Laurel's mother, the house itself, that she has "conspired with silence" and must finally shout both "Abuse!" and "Love!" And indeed Fay arrives at this moment, her return from Texas timed for Laurel's departure (the bridesmaids by now are waiting at the curb to drive Laurel to Jackson). Laurel challenges Fay with the ruined breadboard—

> "It's just an old board, isn't it?" cried Fay.
> "She made the best bread in Mount Salus!"
> "All right! Who cares? She's not making it now."
> "Oh, my mother could see exactly what you were going to do!"

Laurel has judged at last, in rage, and in rage has discovered the order of experience, the mysterious justice of time and understanding, her mother's final accurate desperation—

> Her mother had suffered every symptom of having been betrayed, and it was not until she had died, had been dead long enough to lie in danger of being forgotten and the protests of memory came due, that Fay had ever tripped in. It was not until then, perhaps, that her father himself had ever dreamed of a Fay. For Fay was Becky's own dread . . . Suppose every time her father went on a business trip . . . there had been a Fay.

So memory itself is no longer safe, no "game for the bereaved." The past is never safe because it is never *past*, not while a single mind remembers. Laurel requires revenge. She accuses Fay of desecrating the house, but in vain—as she'd known the night before, Fay does not understand and will not ever, least of all from Laurel (she had used the board for cracking nuts). Fay can only resort to calling Laurel "crazy," to hurtful revelation, an anecdote of

Laurel's mother's last wildness—throwing a bedside bell at a visitor. Laurel raises the breadboard to threaten Fay. Fay has the courage of her ignorance, stands and scornfully reminds Laurel that her friends are waiting outside— "You're supposed to be leaving." Then Fay goes on to claim she'd intended reconciliation, had returned in time for that—". . . we all need to make some allowance for the cranks . . ." Laurel abandons the weapon, one more piece of Fay's inheritance, and hurries to leave, escorted away by her own bridesmaids.

I have summarized at such length because it's my experience, both as reviewed writer and teacher, that even a trained reader (especially trained readers) cannot be relied on to follow the action, the linked narrative, of any long story, especially of a story whose action is interior. (Ask ten trained readers what happens in *Heart of Darkness*—not what are the symbols or controlling metaphors but, simply, who does what to whom and why? Who knows what at the end? *Then* you'll see some darkness.) Also because to summarize *The Optimist's Daughter* is to demonstrate how perfectly the meaning inheres in the form and radiates from it. Nothing is applied from outside or wrenched; the natural speed of the radiation—action into meaning—is never accelerated (with the possible exception of the trapped bird's escape); and no voice cries "Help!" at its lethal rays—lethal to illusion, temporary need.

But the length of a summary has left me little space to discuss important details—to mention only two: first, the language (which in its stripped iron efficiency, its avoidance of simile and metaphor, bears almost no resemblance to the slow dissolving impressionism, relativism of the stories in *The Bride of the Innisfallen*; that was a language for describing what things are *not*, for intensifying mystery; this is a language for stating facts) and, second, the story's apparent lack of concern with Mississippi's major news at the time of the story—the civil rights revolution. Its apparent absence is as complete as that of the Napoleonic wars from Jane Austen. And for the same reason, surely—it is not what this story is about. When Judge McKelva's old law partner says of him at the funeral, "Fairest, most impartial, sweetest man in the whole Mississippi Bar," no irony seems intended nor can honestly be extracted. (I've stressed *apparent* absence because any story which so ruthlessly examines blindness is "about" all the forms of blindness; and if any reader is unprepared to accept the fact that in all societies at all times good and evil coexist in all men and can, under certain conditions of immense complexity, be compartmentalized, quarantined from one another within the same heart, then this story's not for him. So much the worse for him— neither will most art be.)

What I cannot skimp is my prior suggestion that the puzzlement or

contented suspension of onlookers in Miss Welty's earlier fiction vanishes in
The Optimist's Daughter, that the end clarifies. The stance of the onlooker—
forced on him and/or chosen—is confirmed as the human stance which can
hope for understanding, simple survival. The aims of participation are union,
consolation, continuance—doomed. Laurel (who might well be the adult of
the girl in "A Memory" or even of Laura in *Delta Wedding*) might so easily
have left us with a last word fierce as her mother's. She might have said,
"Show me a victor, an *actor* even." Or worse, she might have laughed.

For there is at the end, each time I've reached it, a complicated sense
of joy. Simple exhilaration in the courage and skill of the artist, quite separate
from the tragic burden of the action. Joy that a piece of credible life has
been displayed to us fully and, in the act, fully explained (I take Laurel's
understanding to be also the author's and ours; there can be no second
meaning, no resort to attempts to discredit Laurel's vision). And then perhaps
most troubling and most appeasing, the sense that Laurel's final emotion is
joy, that she is now an "optimist" of a sort her father never knew (if not as
she drives away from her home, then tomorrow, back at work)—that the
onlooker's gifts, the crank's, have proved at last the strongest of human
endowments (vision, distance, stamina—the courage of all three); that had
there been any ear to listen, Laurel would almost surely have laughed,
abandoning her weapon (as Milton's God laughs at the ignorance and ruin
of Satan, only God has hearers—the Son and His angels). For Laurel has
been both victim and judge—who goes beyond both into pure creation (only
she has discovered the pattern of their lives—her parents', Fay's, the Chisoms', her friends', her own) and then comprehension, which is always
comic. All patterns are comic—snow crystal or galaxy in Andromeda or
family history—because the universe is patterned, therefore ordered and
ruled, therefore incapable of ultimate tragedy (interim tragedy is comprised
in the order but cannot be the end; and if it should be—universal pain—
then that too is comic, by definition, to its only onlooker). God's vision is
comic, Alpha and Omega.

MALCOLM COWLEY, WALKER PERCY, ROBERT PENN WARREN

Three Tributes

MALCOLM COWLEY

Others having spoken of the work, I should like to pay a brief tribute to the personal qualities of Eudora Welty. Gentle, unruffled, unassuming, kind, she is an unusual figure in a profession that is marked too often by the dry clash of unsheathed vanities. "Isn't she nice!" other writers always say of her. Her writing is nice, too, but in the older sense of the word, that is, fastidious, scrupulous, marked by delicate discrimination, but never weak or paltering. Let us salute her achievements in literary style and personal style, in prose and life.

WALKER PERCY

What is most valuable about Eudora Welty is not that she is one of the best living short story writers. (It was startling that when I tried to think of anybody else as good, two women and one man came to mind, all three Southerners: Katherine Anne Porter, Caroline Gordon and Peter Taylor.) Nor is it that she is a women of letters in the old sense, versatile and many-voiced in her fiction and as distinguished in criticism. No, what is valuable is that she has done it in a place. That is to say, she has lived all her life in a place and written there and the writing bears more than an accidental relation to the place. Being a writer in a place is not the same as being a banker in a place. But it is not as different as it is generally put forward as being. It is of more than passing interest that Eudora Welty has always lived

From *Shenandoah* 20 (Spring 1969). © 1969 by Washington and Lee University. Originally entitled "Five Tributes."

in Jackson and that the experience has been better than endurable. This must be the case, because if it hadn't been, she'd have left. Although I do not know Eudora Welty, I like to imagine that she lives very tolerably in Jackson. At least she said once that she was to be found "underfoot in Jackson." What does such an association between a writer and a town portend? It portends more, I would hope, than such and such a trend or characteristic of "Southern literature." For Eudora Welty to be alive and well in Jackson should be a matter of considerable interest to other American writers. The interest derives from the coming need of the fiction writer, the self-professed alien, to come to some terms with a community, to send our emissaries, to strike an entente. The question is: how can a writer live in a place without either succumbing to angelism and haunting it like a ghost or being "on," playing himself or somebody else and watching to see how it comes out? The answer is that it is at least theoretically possible to live as one imagines Eudora Welty lives in Jackson, practice letters—differently from a banker banking but not altogether differently—and sustain a relation with one's town and fellow townsmen which is as complex as you please, even ambivalent, but in the end life-giving. It is a secret relationship but not necessarily exploitative. One thinks of Kierkegaard living in Copenhagen and taking great pride in making an appearance on the street every hour so that he would be thought an idler. But it is impossible to imagine Kierkegaard without Copenhagen. Town and writer sustain each other in secret ways. Deceits may be practiced. But one is in a bad way without the other.

The time is coming when the American novelist will tire of his angelism—of which obsessive genital sexuality is the most urgent symptom, the reaching out for the flesh which has been shucked—will wonder how to get back into a body, live in a place, at a street address. Eudora Welty will be a valuable clue.

ROBERT PENN WARREN

It is easy to praise Eudora Welty, but it is not easy to analyze the elements in her work that make it so easy—and such a deep pleasure—to praise. To say that may, indeed, be the highest priase, for it implies that the work, at its best, is so fully created, so deeply realized, and formed with such apparent innocence that it offers only itself, in shining unity.

But some nagging curiosity about the *why* of things may persist, and if it does, that, too, may be a kind of tribute, a tribute to the implicatory power of the work, to its depth. This curiosity persists for me, and when I puzzle the question, I come up with something like this. Eudora Welty's vision of—

her feeling for—the world is multiple. She never, even when she nods, sinks into what Blake called "the single vision and Newton's sleep." There is a strain of merciless mirth, as in "The Petrified Man" or "Why I Live at the P.O." There is a strain of tenderness and pathos, a sense of what life is like for all the lost and rejected ones in the world. There is a strain of violence, muted but compelling, an awareness of the potential terror in experience. There is a strain of fantasy which may eventuate in tales not so different in dimension from those of Hawthorne, sometimes giving us the teasing charm of work like "The Wide Net." But her imagination give us, too, a tough and beautiful poetry of the thing-ness of things, of the "real."

I am not saying that she writes many different kinds of stories—though there is considerable variety of her work. I am saying that in her work these various impulses work themselves out in differing combinations and with different emphases.

What makes her work hang together? What keeps it from appearing as a kind of anarchy of talent, an irresponsible glitter, like a slowly turning kaleidoscope? I am about to answer "temperament"—though aware that the word may seem to beg the question. So I want to elaborate a little and say that it is a temperament so strongly and significantly itself that it can face the multiplicity of the world. Art is the appropriate expression of such a temperament—art not as an escape from the incoherence of the world, but as a celebration of its richness—secure in an instinctive trust of self and in the knowledge that only out of the strong shall come forth sweetness.

CLEANTH BROOKS

Eudora Welty and the Southern Idiom

Like any other writer, Eudora Welty speaks and writes the Queen's English, or, if you prefer, now that a Southerner occupies the White House, the President's English; and she is the author of works that make use of the resources of our language at its highest level. The interior life, the world of fantasy and imagination, is the subject matter of much of her fiction. Robert Penn Warren, in a fine essay on her earlier work, has stressed her treatment of the theme of isolation and her concern for characters cut off from the world, alienated and locked into their own subjectivity. I acknowledge this important aspect of her work and doubtless it will be fully discussed in some of the papers that we are to hear later at this symposium. But what I want to stress this afternoon is Miss Welty's treatment of the folk culture of the South. She evidently knows that culture intimately, and her stories make it plain that she is fascinated by it. Nevertheless, she views it with an artist's proper detachment. Like the good artist that she is, she never condescends to the folk culture or treats it with anything less than full artistic seriousness.

I repeat: she knows its language thoroughly. She has got the vocabulary right and she has caught perfectly the accent, the intonation, and the very rhythms. But I wonder whether you who sit before me now take this folk speech seriously enough—not that many of you have not heard it all your lives. But life-long familiarity may have bred contempt, or at least indifference. Allow me, then, a few minutes' digression in order to try to excite your interest in what lies, if not all around you, at least not too far away, either in time or in space.

The typical language of the Southern folk culture is, within limits, a dialect of considerable force and vitality. Morevoer, it is not a deformed and

---

From *Eudora Welty: A Form of Thanks.* © 1979 by the University Press of Mississippi.

debased version of the standard language—that is to say, a bastard offspring
of "correct" English. Its roots go far back into the past, for it derives from
a speech long extant in the British countryside. How can I make this point
forcefully and yet concisely? It occurs to me that the best way in which to
do this is to read to you from a little book published in 1860. The book, by
the way, is something of a rarity. No copy exists in that vast repository of
books, the British Museum, or, as it has now been renamed, the British
Library.

The author of this little book, a sound scholar of his own time, decided
to present the King James Version of The Song of Solomon as it would have
been pronounced by the dialect speakers of his native country. Here is the
way it goes.

> 1 De song of songs, dat is Solomon's.
>
> 2 Let him kiss me wud de kisses of his mouth; for yer love
> is better dan wine.
>
> 3 Cause of de smell of yer good intments, yer naum is lik
> intment tipped out; derefore de maidens love ye.
>
> 4 Drâh me: we wull run âhter ye: de king has brung me
> into his chambers; we wull be glad and be jobal in ye; we wull
> remember yer love more dan wine; de upright love ye.
>
> 5 I be black, but comely, O ye dâhters of Jerusalem; as de
> tents of Kedar, as de hangins of Solomon.
>
> 6 Look not upan me, cause I be black, cause de sun has
> shoun upan me; my mother's childun was mad wud me; dey
> maüd me kipper of de vineyards; but my own vineyard I han't
> kipt.

So run the first six verses of Chapter I. Let me conclude with a few
verses of the last chapter.

> 6 Set me lik a seal pon yer heart, lik a seal pon yer arm,
> for love is as strong as death, jalousy is as cruel as de graüv: de
> coals of it be coals of fire, dat has a most out-de-way flaüm.
>
> 7 Evers'much water caunt squench love, nor de floods caunt
> drawnd it: ef a man wud give all he's got in his house for love,
> it ud be looked upan as naun at all.
>
> 8 We've got a liddle sister, an she han't got no brestes; what
> shull we do for our sister when de dee comes dat she's spoke for?
>
> . . .
>
> 14 Make haüst, my beloved, an be lik a roe or a young hart
> from de mountains of spices.

Does some of this sound familiar to you? Doesn't it remind you of a certain Southern dialect? May not a few of the pronunciations be your very own today? I, for example, tend to say *liddle*, not *little*, a word in which my Yankee friends at Yale are careful to preserve the *t*, whereas I, Southern fashion, turn it into a *d*. I also call attention to the fact that the author of this little book has carefully marked words like *made*, *grave*, and *haste* to indicate a sound like that of the so-called Southern drawl—which isn't really a drawl but the addition of an extra vowel so that nearly every long vowel becomes a dipthong.

What is the dialect used in this little book? That of the county of Sussex, only some forty or fifty miles distant from London. Now, if the country people of Sussex were pronouncing the language in this fashion in 1860, they presumably pronounced it at least this broadly in 1660, some two hundred years earlier, when the great immigration to America was going on, not only from Sussex, of course, but from the neighboring counties to the east and to the west. Surely, many of those who came to the Southern states must have spoken dialects of this general type—that is, variants of the dialects of the southern end of the island of Great Britain.

Now, changes undoubtedly went on after the colonists arrived on these shores. Dialects from different counties of the old country must have jostled against each other, and some of their peculiarities were lost. Education later had its influence. Those whites who had been saying *de*, *dat*, and *derefore*—and I conjecture that a good many must have—began to say *the*, *that*, and *therefore*. But a good many of the black people, who had, perforce, to learn their English from white English speakers, continued to use the *d-* forms because they were for a long time deprived of formal education and so retained the pronunciation they had first learned.

Now let me pause to make plain what I am *not* saying. I am not asserting that the Southern dialect is simply the Sussex dialect or other county dialects transported intact to these shores. As I have said, changes occurred on this side of the Atlantic over the centuries. New words were added from other languages. There was evidently a good deal of innovation, especially in vocabulary. So the assertion that I am making here is really a rather modest one: namely, that the *pronunciation* of the speech of the American South was rather heavily colored by forms from the county dialects of southeastern and southwestern England, and I would add that some *standard* English pronunciations of the seventeenth and eighteenth centuries, pronunciations which died out in England, continued to flourish in America. Unfortunately, we just don't know enough about the development of the American regional dialects to be very specific about the precise details of that development. But the basic derivation of our Southern *pronunciation* of English from the dialects of the southern counties of England seems inescapable.

In any case, the acuteness of Miss Welty's ear for dialect is astonishing. For example, I had for years thought that I was alone in having noticed that many Southerners pronounce *isn't* as *idn't* and *wasn't* as *wadn't*, turning the standard *z* sound into a *d*. That, by the way, is a very out-of-the-way development. *P*'s easily change into *b*'s, or *f*'s into *v*'s, or *t*'s into *d*'s, but a sibilant turned into a dental stop is rare indeed. Again, this peculiar pronunciation of *isn't* and *wasn't* is found, and apparently found only, here in the southern United States and in some of the southern counties of England. Imagine my surprise, therefore, to discover in reading "The Petrified Man" that Miss Welty had unerringly picked it up and recorded it, and for good measure had elsewhere recorded another curious *z* to *d* shift, one that I failed to notice—*business* pronounced *bidness*.

Now, I'm not trying to turn Miss Welty into a dialect specialist, much less a scientific phonetician. She has had far more important business in hand than that. But her grasp of the Southern dialect does have its importance for her literary artistry, and that is one point I have wanted to establish. And I have wanted to accomplish something else: to get this audience to take more interest in Southern speech, particularly in that of the plain people of the South, and to respect it as having historical roots that go far back, deep into the English past. If you can think of the speech of the plain people of the South as being something other than a corruption of correct English and can become aware of the continuity of their speech with the language of Chaucer and Shakespeare, you may be better prepared to understand the respect for this vigorous folk dialect which Miss Welty exhibits in so much of her writing.

So much for my references to pronunciation, but I should point out that pronunciation is the least part of Miss Welty's interest and concern. She is far more interested in matters of vocabulary and of metaphor and idiom. She means to bring Southern folk speech alive on the page in all of its color, vigor, and raciness.

The finest instances of her handling of the speech of the Southern folk are to be found in *The Ponder Heart*, *Losing Battles*, and *The Optimist's Daughter*. They constitute at least the great sustained examples of her rendition of that speech. But I'm not forgetting some of her short stories—for example, "Why I Live at the P.O." or that wonderful story, "The Petrified Man."

The action of this last-named story is set in a small town. The speech that we hear there is raffish and vulgar in a pseudo-citified way. It is the chitchat of a rather cheap beauty parlor. The language in *Losing Battles*, on the other hand, is not at all vulgar or cheap. The characters in *Losing Batles* are rustic and unlettered, but each of them is as genuine as a handmade hickory kitchen chair, not in the least common or trashy.

On the other hand, the beautician named Leota who dominates "The Petrified Man" is wonderfully vulgar, but she is also wonderful to listen to in the same way as are some of the shabbier characters in Chaucer's *Canterbury Tales*. If the beauty parlor as the town headquarters for female gossip has cheapened and coarsened Leota's mind and spirit, her moving into town has not yet quite sapped the vitality of her country-bred language. It surges on triumphantly, and Eudora Welty has reproduced Leota's manner to a nicety. Listen to her on the subject of Lady Evangeline, the mind reader: When a customer asks "Who's Lady Evangeline?" Leota is not slow to come up with an answer.

> Well, it's this mind reader they got in the freak show. Was real good. Lady Evangeline is her name, and if I had another dollar I wouldn't do a thing but have my other palm read. She had what Mrs. Pike said was the "sixth mind" but she had the worst man-icure I ever saw on a living person.

In Leota's mind, a certain professional knowingness lives happily along-side utter naiveté. Does Leota really think that a reading of her other palm wouldn't duplicate the reading of the first? Or does she credit herself with a split personality—two quite different minds to be read, one attached to her right hand, the other to her left? Yet maybe Leota is—in a certain crazy way—right after all. Though Lady Evangeline calls herself a mind reader, what she actually reads are palms. In any case, Leota, as a beautician, can spot a poor manicure right across the room. The "worst manicure [she] ever saw on a living person" belong to a woman who is constantly holding in her hand other people's hands.

Eudora Welty's delicate but powerful grasp of the speech of the country people of the South reminds me of what William Butler Yeats, the great Irish poet, remarked in an essay entitled "What Is 'Popular Poetry'?" Yeats carefully distinguished between popular poetry and the true poetry of the folk. Popular poetry, he argued, did not, in spite of all its pretenses, issue from the folk at all. Yeats saw it as essentially a middle-class phenomenon, and the typical "popular" poets were Longfellow, Mrs. Felicia Hemans, and the Sir Walter Scott of *Marmion* and *The Lady of the Lake*. The audience to which this popular poetry appealed was composed of "people who have unlearned the unwritten tradition which binds [together] the unlettered . . . [but] who have not learned the written tradition which has been established

on the unwritten." It's very acute discrimination. Popular poetry in this bad
sense appeals to people who have discarded the age-old oral tradition of the
folk ballad and the folk tale. But in repudiating the heritage of the unlettered,
they have not taken the trouble to master the written tradition of the truly
literate reader. Yeats believed that both the oral and the written tradition
could be expected to yield literature. What he denied was that true literature
ever could issue from that group which was neither one nor the other—
writers who wrote for readers only superficially literate, readers who wanted
their poems and stories clear and plain, easily moralized and easily
understood.

Yeats here is not condescending to the literature of the folk. "There is
only one kind of good poetry," he insists, and poetry both of the oral *and*
the written tradition belong to it, for both are "strange and obscure, and
unreal to all who have not understanding." Those ignoramuses who have
not understanding are members of that in-between group who demand "manifest logic" and "clear rhetoric." Television addicts and subscribers to the
Book-of-the-Month take notice! The ghost of William Butler Yeats is looking
very sternly at you.

I believe that Yeats has a genuine point here, and one that applies to
the folk literature of the South. The Southern folk culture is still vibrant
and alive, and affords rich material for the gifted professional writer who
respects it and knows how to make use of it. The dangers are two: first, that
the writer will exploit folk material for cheap laughs and so produce merely
a succession of Little Abners and Daisy Mays, caricatures that are appropriate
to an Al Capp comic strip but have no place in genuine literature. The other
danger is that the folk speaker in actual life, the country-bred man or woman
who is steeped in the oral tradition, will become merely half-educated and
lose the values that he now possesses without acquiring the virtues of true
literacy.

I hope that I am properly understood here: I am not for keeping the
country folk on reservations as if they were an endangered species to be
preserved for the amusement and entertainment of us well-educated people.
Quite the contrary: I would like to see the country-bred attain to full literacy
and a full spiritual development. But the danger is that in a world of cheap
and often meretricious reading matter and television programs they will not
attain full mental and spiritual development at all. They will more likely
lose the genuine tradition that they have without gaining the riches of the
great tradition.

Leota, I would judge, has already picked up some of the triviality and
cheapness of her rather scruffy beauty parlor life. But she still keeps her

hold on a live and vigorous tradition of expressive English. If it is not quite what Spenser called "a well of English undefiled," neither is it yet a mere mud puddle.

Wanda Fay, in *The Optimist's Daughter*, by contrast, has been severely damaged. But perhaps she was flawed from the first. To have come out of a folk culture is no guarantee of virtue. Indeed, one of the fundamental religious tenets of the Southern folk culture is the doctrine of Original Sin: nobody is saved naturally; we have all fallen and come short. At all events, Wanda Fay is clearly a shallow little vulgarian.

She marries the widower, Judge McKelva, a man of some distinction, much older than herself, a man who comes from a very different stratum of society. When the Judge dies, Wanda Fay creates a scene at the funeral. She leans over her husband's coffin and cries out, "Oh, Hon, get up, get out of there." In dying, the Judge has somehow betrayed her, and she screams, "Oh, Judge, how could you be so unfair to me?" Someone tries to calm her and urges her just to bid him goodbye with a farewell kiss. Instead, she fights off the friends surrounding her and throws "herself forward across the coffin onto the pillow, driving her lips without aim against the face under hers," and is dragged "back into the library," screaming.

> "Well, you've done fine so far, Wanda Fay. I was proud of you today. And proud for you. That coffin made me wish I could have taken it right away from him and given it to Roscoe." [Roscoe is her dead husband.]
>
> "Thank you," said Fay. "It was no bargain and I think that showed . . . ."
>
> "You drew a large crowd, too," said Sis.
>
> "I was satisfied with it," said Fay.

Judge McKelva's only child, his grown-up daughter Laurel, is appalled. Later on, after her young stepmother's departure. Laurel's friends feel free to comment on Wanda Fay's conduct, and they do so. But Miss Adele Courtland, the school teacher and sister of the physician who attended Judge McKelva, tries to be charitable.

> "Strangely enough [she said], I think that carrying-on was Fay's idea of giving a sad occasion its due. She was rising to it, splendidly—By her lights! . . . She wanted nothing but the best for her husband's funeral, only the most expensive casket, the most choice cemetery plot, . . . and . . . the most broken-hearted, most distraught behavior she could manage on the part of the widow."

But her interpretation is not acclaimed. Miss Tennyson finally remarks savagely, "I could have broken her neck."

We shall miss the point, however, if we conclude that Miss Welty means to disparage the yeoman whites as a class or even the lowly poor white. Wanda Fay is really awful: "common poor white trash" would scarcely seem too harsh a term to apply to her, and Wanda Fay's sister and mother are of the same stripe. But Miss Welty does not allow that even this family is wholly corrupted. Wanda Fay's grandfather, old Mr. Chisom, seems genuine enough, a decent old man, who had gone to considerable trouble to pay his respects. He arrives late for the funeral because he had had to make an all-night trip by bus. He has sat up most of the night shelling the prize pecans he is bringing to Laurel as a gift. He didn't mind the labor of shelling the pecans, he tells her; it was a way of keeping himself awake on the bus trip.

There is also little Wendell Chisom, attending the funeral in his cowboy suit. He sports a pair of holsters containing two toy pistols. Laurel, responding to the child's bewilderment and innocence, feels an impulse "to reach out for him, put her arms around him—to guard him. He was like a young, undriven, unfalsifying, unvindictive Fay."

The best testimony, however, to Miss Welty's respect for and even a certain affection for the genuine folk culture is to be found in *The Ponder Heart* and especially in *Losing Battles*. *The Ponder Heart* is comic, even merrily absurd; *Losing Battles*, though it has its own comedy too, and closes with a qualified happy ending, is more deeply grounded on the inexorable facts of life.

The Ponder Heart is in its presentation one long unbroken monologue issuing from the lips of Edna Earle Ponder, the proprietress of the Beulah Hotel, the main hostelry of Clay, Mississippi. Let no one object that Edna Earle isn't really one of the folk since she has deserted the countryside and become a townie, subject to some of the corruptions of a citified existence. In the first place, Clay is evidently not very much of a town. It merges easily into the country. The inhabitants of Clay are, to all intents and purposes, as Edna Earle would say, still country people. I admit that she is capable of amiably putting someone down by advising him not to be "so small town." But that is part of the joke. If Clay isn't small town, what town is?

In any case, Edna Earle is uncommonly good company. In her exuberance and in her earthy complacency, she reminds me of Chaucer's Wife of Bath. Like the Wife, Edna Earle is perceptive, on occasion even witty, and always the complete mistress of her own little domain. And like the wife of Bath, how Edna Earle can talk! It is interesting to note what she says to her auditor as the narrative opens.

"*You're* here [that is, here at the Beaulah Hotel, she tells him] because your car broke down, and I'm afraid you're allowing a Bodkin to fix it." [The Bodkin family is obviously in Edna Earle's black book.]

Is this remark a warning or a bit of commiseration? In any case, the man with the disabled car seems willing to let the subject drop; he has evidently picked up a magazine or a book, for Edna Earle immediately says: "And listen: if you read, you'll just put your eyes out. Let's just talk."

Edna Earle compels a hearing even as Coleridge's Ancient Mariner did, and like the Ancient Mariner she evidently does all the talking. Whether her victim eventually leaves her as a wiser and a sadder man, we do not learn. But one fact becomes plain: Edna Earle is clearly not a devotee of Yeats's written tradition. Reading just puts your eyes out. She is a high priestess of the oral tradition.

Someone has said that the many clichés and trite expressions that Miss Welty's characters, including Edna Earle, employ "reflect unimaginative thinking and [a] distrust of the new." To give an example, Edna Earle rattles off glib comparisons such as "she was shallow as they come," she was as "pretty as a doll," "he ate me out of house and home," "good as gold," could "cut your hair to a fare-ye-well," "didn't bother her one whit," and so on. These are well-worn phrases, but all oral art makes use of such formulas and couldn't proceed without them. The English and Scottish folk ballads are filled with such conventional phrases, and even Homer in his *Iliad* uses over and over again such formulas as "the rosy-fingered dawn" and "the fleet-footed Achilles."

Another critic may ask: "Don't her people often use literary words that are quite out of character with their usual vocabulary?" For example, Edna Earle Ponder conjectures that "Maybe anybody's heart would *quail*, trying to keep up with Uncle Daniel's." Jack Renfro asks his father, "What brought you forth?" and tells Judge and Mrs. Judge Moody that "Banner is still my realm." How did these bookish terms, "quail" and "realm," not to mention "brought forth," get into the folk speech? Easy as pie, as Edna Earle would say. Right out of the King James Version of the Bible, or out of the hymns sung every Sunday morning in the Methodist and Baptist churches. If we need a reminder of the latter source. Miss Welty makes verses from the popular evangelical hymns resound again and again through the pages of *Losing Battles*.

A moment ago I mentioned the use of the word *whit* to mean a particle, a tiny bit. I remember my own mother's frequent use of the term. But just to be sure of the status of this word, I took the precaution of looking it up in the *Oxford English Dictionary*. It is a good English term going back as early as the fifteenth century, but the *OED* characterizes it as "now archaic or literary"; and this designation, it appears to me, is an excellent description of much of the vocabulary of the Southern folk speech such as one finds in the pages of Eudora Welty. The words are pleasantly out of date and may in fact sound "literary" just because they are not the ordinary speech of everyday as we hear it typically on national television or read it in *Time* magazine.

So much for what I trust may be my last digression. It's high time to get back to Edna Earle. Eudora Welty is an artist, and she has permitted Edna Earle to be a kind of artist too. In proof, listen to Edna Earle's summary account of her addle-pated Uncle Daniel's marriage to Miss Teacake Magee.

> At any rate, Uncle Daniel and Miss Teacake got married. I just asked her for recipes enough times, and told her the real secret of cheese straws—beat it three hundred strokes—and took back a few unimportant things I've said about the Baptists. The wedding was at the Sistrunks', in the music room, and Miss Teacake insisted on singing at her own wedding—sang "The Sweetest Story Ever Told."

This is masterly.

Losing Battles is Miss Welty's most profound and most powerfully moving account of the folk society. In it we listen to a whole clan gathered for the birthday of its matriarch, great-grandmother Vaughn, and we hear them talk from the dawn of one day to near midnight and later on into the afternoon of the following day. It is wonderfully rich and exuberant talk and there are a variety of voices: male and female, gentle and quiet or aggressive and domineering, querulous and argumentative or ironic and conciliatory; but they are all voices of the folk and speak the characteristic folly or wisdom, joy or melancholy, of such a community.

In emphasizing the wonderful talk to be found in this novel—its quality and its quantity—I may have given the impression that nothing happens—that the novel is all just talk. Nothing could be further from the truth. All kinds of things happen. There are hairbreadth escapes from violent death, turnings of the table in which the judge who had sentenced Jack Renfro to the penitentiary turns up, through a curious set of happenings, at Granny Vaughan's birthday party for the concluding banquet and actually spends the night under the same roof that shelters Jack Renfro on his first night home after returning from the penitentiary. Mysteries are unraveled: Jack's bride, Gloria, the orphan who does not know who her parents were, has the puzzle worked out for her and discovers that she is her husband's first cousin. But as she is welcomed into the clan as blood-kin, no longer just an in-law, it is revealed that Mississippi has passed a law against first cousins marrying each other. Gloom descends at once. Will Jack, just home, have to return to the penitentiary because of this newly discovered offense? He had earlier had to give up his bride after only one night of married bliss. Now that he has held her in his arms once again, will he be snatched away? Yet it is his old antagonist, Judge Moody, who enables him to escape this new threat of the law.

I am reminded here of some amusing anecdotes that my wife recently passed on to me—anecdotes of which she was reminded by reading *Losing Battles*. During World War II, when she worked at a small war plant, she acquired a secretary from East Feliciana Parish, Louisiana, a young woman probably from just such a family as the Renfros. The secretary had obviously "risen," as had Jack Renfro's young wife, Gloria. She was not in the least self-conscious about her background, though now living a more sophisticated life in Baton Rouge.

During the Christmas season, she spoke of her pleasure in seeing her two young brothers, home on leave after having been away for some months. Not in the Army, it turned out, but in the penitentiary—for what offense I don't know, but probably something not very shame-making. They had brought along with them an obligation—and not just the obligation to return to the penitentiary when leave was over. Their particular task—one for which presumably they possessed talent—was the care of the penitentiary bloodhounds. They had done such a good job in taking care of, and possibly training, these dogs that they had been required to take the bloodhounds along on Christmas leave and care for them at home. The fact that the Louisiana State Penitentiary is located in the same parish in which the boys lived makes the happening more logical. They probably knew the warden or other employees, probably had uncles and cousins on the staff; so the particulars of their Christmas leave were easily and naturally arranged.

Another anecdote from my wife: the secretary wanted to take an aspirin; yet the only source of water was the office drinking fountain—no glasses or paper cups. She was at a loss. My wife suggested that she put the aspirin in her mouth and then drink like a chicken. There was instant communication and the aspirin were successfully swallowed.

But back to *Losing Battles*. Action, indeed! Far from being simply a talky novel, *Losing Battles* is practically a melodrama—and thus far I have not even mentioned the violent physical action, such as the fist fights that occur or the wonderful episode in which Judge Moody's car runs off the road and sits perched on an eminence so perilous that it takes truly superhuman efforts to get it down once more into the road.

The truth of the matter is that *Losing Battles* is in spirit a kind of Tall Tale of the Old Southwest. Indeed, the action is so violent and some of the coincidences so improbable that it needs its folk language and sayings and ways for the actions depicted to pass muster as credible. Pass muster they do, for by virtue of its folk characters and the language they speak, the novel strikes the reader as being itself a kind of folk tale—bardic, outrageously strange, almost epic in its happenings.

A second qualification that I want to make is this: in spite of the seriousness with which Eudora Welty takes this folk culture, she does not sentimentalize it. She does not make it too good to be true. If the clan loyalties of the Beechams and the Renfros are admirable and excite the envy of us modern readers who tend to be alienated, lacking in family ties, and lonely in our unhappy self-sufficiency, Miss Welty makes it plain that the pressure of this great extended Renfro family can be suffocating. Gloria wants to have Jack to herself. During his long absence she has tried to find a little privacy in this busy, cluttered, almost too tightly related tribe. Even after she has had revealed to her that her father was a Renfro too, she yearns to get away from Jack's vast family. As the novel ends, she is still saying: "And some day, some day, yet, we'll move to ourselves. And there'll be just you and me and Lady May." Lady May is their baby girl.

This counter note, this glimpse at the other side of the matter, is the necessary pinch of salt. The strength of family ties is touching, and the loyalties of the clan may well rouse in the modern a certain homesickness for a world that many of us have lost. But Miss Welty is not writing a tract in defense of the extended family. Rather, she is dramatizing such a family, and in doing so she is telling the truth about it. The virtues are there, but the Renfros have the defects of their virtues.

One of their defects is a kind of naiveté. Jack is goodhearted, impulsive, loyal, essentially kindly, though very jealous of what he regards as his masculine honor. It is his naiveté which first gets him into trouble, and in the course of the day and a half that we watch Jack's actions we see that his guileless simplicity continues to get him into trouble. His young wife Gloria is quite aware of this. She feels more protective of her husband than even he feels protective of her, for she realizes that he is far more vulnerable. He allows people to goad him into foolish actions. He is really incapable of taking care of himself.

Some of Jack's aunts and uncles and cousins are more worldly-wise than he. Yet in a sense Jack Renfro's special vulnerability does hint at the vulnerability of the folk society itself. It is genuine, sincere, strong in integrity, resolute, and capable of suffering without whining. But its chief virtues are those that can be handed down in a simple and basically unlettered society. Book learning, after all, does provide virtues too—very important ones—and these the Renfros tend to lack.

The folk society is a bit skittish about book learning. It is natural that it should eye with a certain suspicion the world of books and the rhetoric of false grandiloquence that goes with it. A little learning is indeed a dangerous thing, and on this point the suspicion manifested by the folk makes a certain sense. But the folk are even more afraid of profound learning—for this smacks of a strange and unfamiliar world filled with abstractions.

Miss Welty has made this point subtly but very forcibly in *Losing Battles*. Though we never see Miss Julia Mortimer, the school teacher who has made her impact on so many lives in Banner, the bailiwick of the Renfros, her name comes up again and again throughout the novel. She has just died. Indeed, her funeral is held the day after the Renfro reunion, and the whole community repairs to the cemetery to witness her burial. Judge Moody and his wife attend it, and so do Jack Renfro and Gloria. Gloria had in fact been a protégé of Miss Julia's and had come to the Banner community as the mistress of its one-room school. It was in the school that she met Jack, an overage pupil, and fell in love with him, married him, and gave up the career of a teacher, the profession to which Miss Julia had hoped Gloria would devote her life.

Miss Julia had been a great teacher and a formidable power in the community. Judge Moody, for example, had been one of her pupils, and several of her best pupils had gone on to glory in the great world outside. On the day of her funeral men of more than merely local fame had returned to Banner to pay their respects. Yet in the talk that we hear from the Renfro clan, we note a certain uneasiness and suspicion. They respect Miss Julia and even take some pride in having weathered their experiences in her schoolroom. But they think of schooling as a necessary evil, and their awe of Miss Julia is mingled with a certain fear. She was the dedicated priestess of what was for them an arcane mystery. They were never really comfortable with her.

A folk community is usually uneasy in the presence of those who exalt the written word, and in this regard Miss Welty's Banner community is not special. Other Southern writers have made the same point. An excellent example is Peter Taylor's fine story "Miss Leonora When Last Seen." The story is narrated by one of Miss Leonora's former pupils, and in his account of this admirable but formidable woman, who wished to lift her pupils to a higher plane of intellect and achievement, the narrator himself reveals mixed feelings. If in the end he comes down firmly on Miss Leonora's side, his difficulties with her schoolmarm-ism clearly reflect the mixed feelings of the town. In *Losing Battles* this mingling of respect with a certain resentment, and gratitude with fearful apprehension, comes to a head in the person of Gloria. Gloria owes much to Miss Julia, and yet she resents the fact that Miss Julia had not approved her marriage to Jack Renfro. Gloria seems to count herself a brand snatched from the burning, a maiden rescued by her own St. George from the dragon of permanent spinsterhood. Yet, much as she loves her young husband and baby, she resists sinking back into the clannish domesticity of the Beechams and Renfros. She does want her own life as a wife and mother, but not on just any terms.

The suspicion in which any teacher is held by the generality of the folk—particularly their suspicion of the person who means to teach them how to read and write and spell—is not, however, merely Southern. I'm inclined to say that it is All-American. When I meet strangers and they find out that I'm a college professor, they invariably politely ask what I teach. I dread to tell them, for I can predict the chill that will immediately descend. "Gee, English was always my worst subject." Or: "You probably think my pronunciation is awful." Or perhaps, trying to cheer me up: "But you don't talk like an English professor. You sound perfectly natural."

Such is the uneasy truce that is struck between the representatives of the oral and the written traditions. And I can be sympathetic with the fears that plague the child of the oral tradition. He has good reason to guard his innocence. Thus the Renfros, who instinctively flinch from the sophistications of the great world outside, see the school teacher as the prime agent of that studiedly artificial world. As we have earlier remarked, Yeats believed that members of the unwritten oral tradition had cause to be wary in the presence of the evangelists of the printed word. But Yeats knew also that the genuine artist does not threaten the oral tradition of the folk.

The genuine artist, though aware of the limitations of the unwritten tradition, respects it. He appreciates its honesty and its other basic virtues. He knows that these virtues are not really antagonistic to the virtues of the great written tradition. He remembers that Homer, the father of the poetry of Western civilization, was himself a poet of the oral tradition, even though he was to become the very cornerstone of the written tradition.

The genuine artist not only respects and admires the oral tradition; he knows how to use it, how to incorporate it into the written, and thus how to give it an enduring life.

Eudora Welty is just such an artist, for in her work one finds a true wedding of the two diverse but not hostile traditions. It is as such an artist that I salute her on this happy occasion.

DANIELE PITAVY-SOUQUES

Technique as Myth: The Structure
of The Golden Apples

"Tu remarquas, on n'écrit pas, lumineusement, sur champ obscur, l'alphabet
des astres, seul, ainsi s'indique, ébauché ou interrompu; l'homme poursuit noir
sur blanc."

—Mallarmé

Because Eudora Welty herself has suggested that *The Golden Apples* was
more than just another collection of short stories, the structural unity of the
book has puzzled critics over the years. Nearly all the articles dealing with
The Golden Apples as a whole tackle the problem and attempt to solve it by
establishing close parallels between (mostly) Greek mythology and the various characters and incidents in the book. Whether they underline the recurrent myths that can be traced in the different stories or organize all
mythical allusions into echoes and leitmotiv that weave a symphonic web in
the book, these critical approaches remain at the surface of the work. No
doubt, the task is not easy, perhaps chiefly because of the looseness of the
book. It is composed of seven stories, each a brilliant experiment in technique,
and of several different myths—Celtic as well as Greek—collected under a
title that seems to introduce yet another myth. The very multiplicity of these
mythic readings and the lack of a strong unifying device, such as one finds
in *Ulysses*, have marred all attempts at finding a satisfactory structure. Could
not then a different approach be used that would do full justice not only to
this complex work but to the artist herself, who of her generation is perhaps
the most deeply aware of her art?

From *Eudora Welty: Critical Essays*. © 1979 by the University Press of Mississippi.

Content cannot be dissociated from form; the text should be analyzed as a whole. Indeed, its narrative functioning deserves the closest attention since alone it shows the author's intentions. Just as important is the examination of any infraction of the norms established by the work itself, as these infractions help evaluate the esthetic success of the book and give clues that indicate the presence of a less obvious narrative system. The study of the structure of *The Golden Apples* should thus be based on the narration as well as the fiction, and take into account the apparent infractions of its narrative code. Only through such study can one perceive the essential function of myth in the book, thence the deeper meaning of Welty's work.

In *The Golden Apples* Welty very deliberately used what T. S. Eliot called "the mythical method" in his 1923 *Dial* review of *Ulysses*: "It is simply a way of controlling, of ordering, of giving a shape and a significance to the immense panorama of futility and anarchy which is contemporary history. It is a method already adumbrated by Mr. Yeats, and of the need for which I believe Mr. Yeats to have been the first contemporary to be conscious. It is a method for which the horoscope is auspicious." Myth here is technique, imposed on the world of action, shaping our perception and reaction to it. Eliot's comment is further relevant because he gives credit to Yeats for adumbrating this technique and also mentions the horoscope. Both are directly related to the technique used in *The Golden Apples*. That Eudora Welty intended to experiment with the mythical method in a sustained and deliberate way is indicated by the genesis of her work. The first story of the cycle, "June Recital," was originally called "The Golden Apples," and appeared in *Harper's Bazaar* under this title, partly inspired by "The Song of the Wandering Aengus." Yeats's poem was extensively quoted in the first version. This nucleus story was thus under the double parentage of Yeats and Greek myth. Later, it was renamed and the mythical title transferred to designate the collection as a whole—a unique instance in Welty's work, for the three other collections bear the name of one story. As she worked on the various stories of *The Golden Apples*, she realized, as she said, she was "writing about the same people."

The futility of decoding the characters and events of the book according to a strict mythological system becomes evident from the first story. The warning is there, in the title itself, which functions as a signal to indicate a reality beyond the events in the story. "Shower of Gold" heralds the birth of Perseus to any cultivated reader. But on what level? If we remain on the purely factual level, we read in the story nothing more than the birth of the MacLain twins, Randall and Eugene, not the clandestine birth of an only son. And the "quotation" in the text is scant; the world *gold* is not even mentioned: "She looked like more than only the news had come over her. It was like a shower of something had struck her, like she'd been caught out in something bright." Moreover, this title appears as an infraction of the functioning of the story, which rests entirely on the "truth" of King MacLain's visit to his wife on Halloween. Indeed, this title has nothing to do with the fiction if we except the incomplete allusion. (It functions, of course, as a mythical clue for King MacLain, whom we are thus invited to see as the modern counterpart of Zeus. But this belongs to the surface level of the book; story after story, we are told of the amorous exploits of the character.) We must therefore look elsewhere for the function of the title, beyond the single short story, considering this first piece of narrative as part of a whole, and see whether other allusions to Perseus occur in the book.

The hero reappears, again without being named, in the fourth story, "Moon Lake." The parallel is explicit enough never to have left critics in doubt as to the equation of Loch Morrison's bringing Easter back to life after she has fallen into the lake with Perseus' rescuing Andromeda from the sea monster. The reference is quite precise, developed at length and confirmed, so to speak, by the vision of Loch, alone and enjoying his triumph outside his tent as Perseus did after his first victory. But here again, Perseus and Andromeda and their love affair have no part in the plot of the story. What is most impressive is the strong sexual coloration of the life-saving process. We are once more aware that the significance of this episode is on a second level of reality.

Finally, Perseus' slaying Medusa is the object of Virgie Rainey's long meditation in "The Wanderers." The meditation functions no more directly in this narrative than in the other two stories. It should be noted, however, that Virgie's interpretation is rather unorthodox and shakes the commonly accepted views of the myth: "Miss Eckhart had had among the pictures from Europe on her walls a certain threatening one. It hung over the dictionary, dark as that book. It showed Perseus with the head of the Medusa. 'The same thing as Siegfried and the Dragon,' Miss Eckhart had occasionally said, as if explaining second-best. . . . [Virgie] saw the stroke of the sword in three moments, not one. In the three was the damnation—no, only the secret, unhurting because not caring in itself—beyond the beauty and the sword's stroke and the terror lay their existence in time—far out and endless, a constellation which the heart could read over many a night." At this stage we can draw two conclusions. The myth of Perseus is undoubtedly present in *The Golden Apples*, and Welty's use of this myth is highly deliberate, creative. There is another technical difficulty to solve before examining more closely the function of the myth of Perseus: the title of the collection itself.

The quest for the golden apples is very distantly linked to the myth of
Perseus—some late accretions, which critics bent on finding thematic unity
have hunted for and made the most of. But generally speaking, no one
connects Perseus with the golden apples (though he is Heracles' ancestor).
Since the title "Shower of Gold" functions symbolically, we may infer that
the only other title with a mythical connotation, the general title of the
collection, functions in the same way: it would thus refer not to a definite
search but to *any* search. The text corroborates this hypothesis. The title
was at first given to "June Recital," which originally included the full last
stanza of Yeats's poem, with the reference to "the silver apples of the moon,
/ The golden apples of the sun." When Eudora Welty revised she eliminated
the too explicit lines, favoring indirectness to pedantry, the more refined
method of distant allusion to a labored exercise in name dropping. In fact,
she kept the spirit rather than the letter of the poem. And what quest had
Yeats in mind? Several times he pointed out the duality in the myth and
legends about those who live in the waters and can take any shape like "the
little silver trout" which became "a glimmering girl": "The people of the
waters have been in all ages beautiful and changeable and lascivious, or
beautiful and wise and lonely, for water is everywhere the signature of the
fruitfulness of the body and of the fruitfulness of dreams."

Indeed, the search for the apples provides a loose thematic link between
the different short stories. By their Greek and Celtic parentage the golden
fruit represent the artist's attempt at showing the universality of myth—
human desire and longing, at bringing about a new awareness of the fundamental ambivalence of man through a comparison between several worlds.
The brilliant fabric of mythological names and echoes that adorns the surface
of the text functions in this same way. Welty's use of this technical device
is quite original; it is not coincidence or influence but technique. She uses
mythology as deliberate "quotations" from Yeats, Joyce, or T. S. Eliot, with
the resulting effect of implying that she is writing about universal passions
as eternal as *art*, and the created world itself. (Another way of doing it is to
project what takes place on earth into the stars and constellations, whose
names are derived from the myth, what T. S. Eliot implied when he mentioned the horoscope.) This effect of quotation is a means of guaranteeing
the truth of her fiction, just as, paradoxically, this truth is warranted at the
other end, the realistic end, by the list of the characters printed at the
beginning of the book. What is more, these highly sophisticated literary
"quotations" are a means of suggesting that literature is itself the endless
repetition of the same stories. Welty's attitude becomes reflexive, just as
literature, she seems to suggest, is a mirror. She questions her art in the

very moment she is creating it. Somehow, those "quotations" are the play within the play, contesting the story and the genre while functioning within it. They constitute the mirror that Welty holds to her fiction. Perseus does nothing else: the writer *is* Perseus. To the point here is Reynolds Price's superb definition of the artist—not unconnected with *The Golden Apples*, it seems, as it appears in an essay significantly entitled "Dodging Apples": "The central myth of the artist is surely not Narcissus but Perseus—with the artist in all roles, Perseus, Medusa and the mirror-shield." Here, brilliantly summed up, are indeed the elements of the myth—Perseus, Medusa and the mirror-shield.

The centre of this trinity is fascination—Medusa's deadly gaze, or rather fascination defeated, ovrcome by another gaze—Perseus' in the mirror. At the mythic as well as the symbolic level, fascination means death. At the level of human relations, it refers to that spell, that *abus de pouvoir* by which we tend to objectify the other, to make him lose his identity and become a thing, an object. In his phenomenological study of gaze in *L'Etre et le Néant*, Sartre was perhaps the first to show that fascination is central to the problem of the gaze and to the relation of one being to another. Nearly every form of meaningful relation to the other derives from fascination. Prestige likewise reverses the relation of subject-object. It forces the admirer to lose his identity and wish to identify with the object of his admiration. Emptied of his substance, drained of his blood, the contemplator dies, so to speak. There is also the reverse form of fascination, shame, which is self-loathing. Sartre concludes at the end of his chapter on gaze that, beyond the inconciliable duality of our relation to the other, there is the body, apprehended as the purely contingent presence of the other. This apprehension is a particular type of nausea. We can see how seduction and the wish to possess the body of the other are, eventually, another form of fascination with one's own death, what Sartre calls the obscene. That the myth has strong sexual connotation is evident when we look at its development. Originally, a Gorgon was an ugly creature with hissing snakes as hair; she later became a once beautiful woman turned ugly by Hera's jealousy; at the Hellenistic period, she was simply a beautiful young maid whose gaze was deadly.

All the complexities of feelings based on fascination, tearing man between attraction and repulsion, loving and loathing, fulfillment and destruction inform the treatment of human relations in *The Golden Apples*. There is the fascination for an unworthy type—King MacLain, a rascal who brazenly defies all the social and moral conventions in "Shower of Gold" and "The Wanderers." The nausea linked to the flesh and the self as experienced in sex is central to "Sir Rabbit" and "The Whole World Knows." Death also provides a perilous allure in "Moon Lake." In the more complex stories the theme of fascination shapes with infinite subtlety the projection of the self onto the idealized alter-ego, as in "Music from Spain" and "June Recital," which present the most devastating picture of feelings related to this theme.

Perseus is not a "culture hero" in the sense Prometheus and Heracles are culture heroes, that is, the saviors of mankind, the trangressors, the "transformers" who by their heroic action help civilization progress. Perseus' victory is of a more private kind and concerns the terrors of the soul and the agony of the heart rather than the ordering of chaos.

Even if to the painters Perseus must have been the triumphant hero ("The vaunting was what she remembered, that lifted arm"), even if Loch's victory over death swells him with too much pride in the eyes of Nina Carmichael and Jinny Love, Perseus in *The Golden Apples* is above all that most complex character who alone was able to conceive the full horror of Medusa, since he overcame it: "Because Virgie saw things in their time, like hearing them—and perhaps because she must believe in the Medusa equally with Perseus—she saw the strike of the sword in three moments, not one." Those three moments in one represent the utmost fascination and the awareness of it; somehow it is the fascination of the artist himself, as Malraux, before Price, suggested in the preface he wrote for the French translation of *Sanctuary* in 1932: "The deepest fascination, the artist's, draws its strength from its being both the horror and the possibility to conceive it." To this fascination, Eudora Welty gives a personal coloring: "Cutting off the Medusa's head was the heroic act, perhaps, that made visible a horror in life, that was at once the horror in love, Virgie thought—the separateness." Perseus stands for the fascinated become fascinator, the slaying of Medusa for the lover who could grasp the full essence of his beloved only by killing her. The severed head is not only the visible sign of that permanent scandal—death; it is also the visible sign of that other scandal—the destructive power of love, any form of love (of fascination). For it is the essence of fascination, the utmost form of gaze, to become annihilated in the very accomplishment of the transgression it implies. This failed epiphany Eudora Welty calls "separateness." In "A Still Moment" Lorenzo the watcher and Audubon, seer and voyeur, slayer and lover, knew already that fascination is a knowledge and a love that contains in itself the death of all knowledge and love.

The agony of separateness is what most married characters in *The Golden Apples* experience. Whether it be an unfaithful husband ("Shower of Gold"), an unfaithful wife ("The Whole World Knows"), or an inadequate spouse ("Sir Rabbit," "Music from Spain," Mrs. Morrison in "June Recital"), they all feel the unbreachable gulf between what they dream or hope for and the

reality that makes their lives. In "The Wanderers," Virgie Rainey's long
chain of lovers shows that she too has not been able to find fulfillment in
love. Just as excruciating can be the loneliness of thwarted affection, whether
born of unrequited devotion—a maternal love transfer, Miss Eckhart's feelings for Virgie Rainey in "June Recital"—or the result of death, the scan-
dalous distress of the orphaned child ("Moon Lake"), or of the hundred
smaller sorrows daily experienced.

The third constituent of the myth, the mirror, points to the fascination
of Perseus—his awareness of horror and its fascination for him. The place
of desire, the mirror becomes the door to death. A reflection, it is the sign
of the near identity of opposites: "Virgie never saw it differently, never
doubted that all the opposites on earth were close together, love close to
hate, living to dying; but of them all, hope and despair were the closest
blood—unrecognizable one from the other sometimes, making moments double upon themselves, and in the doubling double again, amending but never
taking back."

This endless doubling upon oneself is fascination—again. And this is
true not only of "moments," but of the short stories themselves as structures.
They are built on this endless reflection, which doubles and doubles again.
There are two parts or two movements in each story that are based on the
ambiguity between a real experience and a dreamed one, between asserted
reality and hypothetical reality. (Interestingly, some of Virginia Woolf's
finest stories, like those of Welty, follow this pattern.) In "The Wanderers"
the axis is "the feeling of the double coming-back," as Virgie Rainey experiences it (or the double departure, which is just its reverse, its reflection in
the mirror). Starting from that evident dichotomy, Eudora Welty elaborates
on a most sophisticated play on reflections. Two examples will illustrate the
technique and stress the duality in the composition of the book itself, since
it rests on two major trends, a comic one based on the celebration of the
word—the art of telling—and a tragic one based on vision—the fascination
of the *spectacle*.

The reflection at times functions as the proof of the authenticity of the
object, as in "Shower of Gold." The narrative problem here is the "truth"
of King's visit on Halloween. In the first part, Mrs. Rainey draws a portrait
of King MacLain, a rogue pursuing his amorous career all over the South,
and through her we hear the adoring voice of the community. In the second
part, she tells at length how he was seen at the door of his house on a surprise
visit to his wife, how he thought better of it when circled by his two young
sons disguised for the day, and ran away once more. But these facts cannot
be proved. Apparently, part two illustrates the gossips told in part one and

corroborates them. However, a close study of the narration shows that it is just the reverse: the legend surrounding King MacLain is what makes the aborted visit credible—in the narrative system of the story.

With a more refined composition, based on the alternating voices of Loch Morrison and his sister Cassie, "June Recital" sends back and forth a series of reflections that contribute to the most scathing criticism of human relations in society. The overall effect is that of the play within the play, since for each witness the *spectacle* he sees constitutes the epitome of his vision—a reflected microcosm of his world. To this mirror-effect within each narrative, a more subtle one is added, which provides the structural link between the two parts. The grey dull picture of what seems the preparation for a celebration is followed by the brilliantly colored image of the celebration itself—the recital. We hesitate over the true nature of what we see (which is the reflection? which is the object?), and a new awareness of the tragedy of human relations is born as the second mirror-effect begins to dawn on us. Until we realize we should superimpose the two scenes so as to see the complete picture, we do not fully apprehend the structure—hence the subject of "June Recital." In Loch's narrative, Miss Eckhart's lavish decoration of her studio with "maypole ribbons of newspaper and tissue paper" reads like a black and white snapshot of the June recital narrated in Cassie's part, its negative rather. The relation between the two scenes provides the key to the understanding of the story; in spite of appearances they are very much alike. Just as we see a proliferation of stage properties in part one, part two presents a proliferation of visual elements to the prejudice of musical ones. The empty stage in part one represents a distortion of the spectacle, produced for its sole end without any audience, just as the June recital deprived of its musical end is similarly distorted. The finality of both spectacles is elsewhere. For that one night in the year the ladies of Morgana cooperate with Miss Eckhart to celebrate themselves, in the end, under the pretense of honoring their daughters. Staged by a narcissistic town enamored of its own image, the brilliantly colorful recital derives its deceptive splendor from success and power. It presents the supreme illusion of the town contemplating its social achievement therein. In the other scene, stripped of its false appearances, the studio looks what it is really—an empty stage for a demented puppet. Likewise, Miss Eckhart's loneliness is made visible together with the destructive effect of her love for Virgie; she has been drained of her vital flux by the dazzled gaze she gave her idol-pupil. Thus the two scenes function like Medusa's head and its reflection in the mirror. The reflected head loses its power to fascinate because it is deprived of the deadly glamour. Vulnerability becomes apparent with the emptiness that fascination implies. The reflection is "truer" than the object, and cannot be dissociated from it. When superimposed, the two pictures give an image in relief, so to speak, suggesting the depth of the tragedy of human relations behind the brilliant surface.

The three elements of the myth of Perseus thus correspond to the major themes and techniques of the book: they are present in every story, and each element functions in the same way as it does in the myth. This structure suggests three organizing principles: all the short stories have a plot based on fascination, they are all constructed with a mirror-effect, and the theme of separateness runs throughout the volume. In other words, the narratives that constitute *The Golden Apples* are dramatizations of the functioning of the myth of Perseus—the essential theme of the book, which was discussed at the beginning of this analysis. *The Golden Apples* illustrates what Jean Ricardou called a "theorem" in his study of the critical problems of the Nouveau Roman: "Great narratives can be recognized in that the story they tell is nothing but the dramatization of their own functioning."

The Golden Apples can be read at the ordinary level of dramatic action. It offers then the picture of a microcosm with its passions and frustrations, hate and prejudice, heroes and scapegoats. At a more significant level, it is concerned with the kinds of awareness various minds have of death, which it is man's fate to fear, fight and fool as much and as long as he can. As the protean figure of Death makes his insidious way into every passion, great or small, that seethes in the heart of man, there are thousands of encounters before the final destruction. Man's dignity or heroism is this endless fight against death and all forms of evil, which are forms of death. For this, he has "the pure wish to live." He has love or art: Miss Eckhart "had hung the picture on the wall for herself. She had absorbed the hero and the victim and then, stoutly, could sit down to the piano with all Beethoven ahead of her. With her hate, with her love, and with the small gnawing feelings that ate them, she offered Virgie her Beethoven."

The myth of Perseus is central to Welty's thought from "A Curtain of Green" to *The Optimist's Daughter*. Only in *The Golden Apples*, of which she said that "in a way it is closest to my heart of all my books," has she fully developed it. The mythic method, which she uses again in *Losing Battles*, though quite differently, leaves the fight endless and somewhat unresolved, except by art. "In Virgie's reach of memory a melody softly lifted, lifted of itself. Every time Perseus struck off the Medusa's head, there was the beat of time, and the melody. Endless the Medusa, and Perseus endless." Pursuing her own ceaseless war with time and death, the artist comes to a different compromise in a more classical novel like *The Optimist's Daughter*. The answer is no longer determined by the fixed revolutions of the heavenly bodies, but is inscribed in human time, and relies on that best of man's weapons, memory. A crucible in which man's heart and spirit are purified of desire and remorse, memory becomes the privileged place where the patterns of our lives—any lives—are written and disclosed to the artist, whose creative vision can thus dominate chaos. In *The Golden Apples* the stars are not alone in transcending time in their eternal movement; so do myths, becoming as fixed in their revolving through centuries and cultures as the constellations which bear their names. And so does the work of art, which first explores the depth of the human heart, then stands in black letters against the white page. Gaining immortality, the work of art thus gives the reverse picture of the luminous stars against the black sky, as Mallarmé once wrote. "You noticed, one does not write with light on a dark background; the alphabet of the stars, alone, is marked in this way, uncompleted or interrupted; man pursues black against white."

SEYMOUR GROSS

A Long Day's Living: The Angelic Ingenuities of Losing Battles

" *'Gloria, we won our day,' said Jack.*"
    Losing Battles (1970)

"*It does lie in my nature to praise
and celebrate things.*"
    WELTY, an interview (1972)

There is a sense in which the title of Eudora Welty's major work in the comic mode, *Losing Battles*, is unfortunate. It does seem to sound the note of defeat, as if it were introducing a novel whose epigraph might be Hemingway's "all stories end in death, and he is no true storyteller who does not tell you that"—or some such thing—rather than the affirmative epigraphs I have chosen for this essay. The title would perhaps merit little remark except that I suspect that it has subtly encourage readings of the novel somewhat too somber, readings which tip the novel toward what is known in Shakespearean criticism as "dark comedy." Louise Gossett, for example, calls it a "comedy of loss," in which "Miss Welty keeps us company—both tender and robustious—as we edge along avoiding doom." For me, such a reading misses the essence of Welty's comic vision, which is basically celebrative, joyous, and affirmative ("My natural temperament is one of positive feelings," she remarked in an interview for the *Paris Review*). Her comic fiction, the culmination of which is *Losing Battles*, displays an enchantment with the energy, diversity, and indomitability of what Emerson in less self-conscious times would have capitalized as Life; it bears testimony to a vision which

From *Eudora Welty: Critical Essays*. © 1979 by the University Press of Mississippi.

sees life as skirting free of the social, moral, and philosophical formulations which would command it into shape; it exhibits a reverence for freedom, a condition in which people and their feelings are not fixed, defined, and labelled, where life has preserved something of its dazzling mobility and dramatic variousness. Clearly this is no shallow optimism; for Welty, like the Emerson or Whitman whom she in some general ways resembles, knows the conditions out of which praise and celebration must be won.

I said in an earlier essay that Welty is in the American Transcendentalist comic tradition; the statement has no significance beyond what the analogy might reveal. The nineteenth-century Transcendentalist wrote no fiction and liked very little of it, perhaps because fiction, being the most reality-laden of the literary forms, finds it most difficult to convincingly "earn" a celebrative vision. A depiction of the world we know works against such a vision. It would be hard to imagine a serious novel in which the ringing affirmations of an Emerson or a Whitman in the mouth of a character would not sound ridiculous.

A more useful comparison for *Losing Battles* is to the fiction of Jane Austen, or, rather, to Eudora Welty's reading of the older author in a fine little appreciation she wrote while working on her novel. This is not to suggest "influence" as traditionally defined in literary scholarship. Instead, a kindred spirit recognizes in another writer some of the qualities of her own talent and talks about them. And as is the case with most such "shock of recognition" essays, we learn as much about the recognizer as we do about the recognized. For the reader of *Losing Battles*, Welty's "Jane Austen" can offer some very suggestive insights into the way Welty's novel is to be taken. I think it not too much to suggest that the essay is almost a generalized summary of the informing vision and method of the novel.

Jane Austen's "comic masterpieces" are, for Welty, "wholly affirmative." The "noise" and "commotion" in her pages flow from "a tireless relish of life," which is a rejoicing in the "clamorous joys and griefs" of her characters. Her fictional stage is small in size but drawn exactly to scale. Take one household, add a neighbor, and there is "the full presence of the world"— "Life . . . is instantaneously at hand and astir . . . with news, arrivals, tumult and crises." Austen "was born knowing a great deal," and among the things she knew was "that the unit of everything worth knowing in life is in the family," that "the interesting situations of life can, and notably do take place at home." Her comedies avoid nothing humanly essential for not being tragedies: they too "are nourished at the primary sources." They never deny "the emotions their power," they encompass "the argument of souls," they explore the range of human motives (which "can still be counted on [one's] fingers"), they pertain "to what goes on perpetually in the mind and heart." But the perspective is always comic; that is, "the effect of the whole is still that of proportions kept, symmetry maintained, and the classical form honored—indeed celebrated." Austen's "comic genius" impels a world in which "she sees and defines both sides," presenting them in their turns "in a continuous attainment of balance: moral, esthetic, and dramatic balance." This "symmetry of design," which Welty characterizes as an "angelic ingenuity," is the projection into art of a "generous dispensation of the understanding."

Losing Battles is a family novel written along just such lines. Its spiritual ebullience is the result of Welty's grand understanding of the joys and griefs of her large cast of characters who, do what they will to tip the world, cannot upset its balance. There is something in the universe which does not like a fall—call it the life force or the natural order or whatever. This impulse is most obviously and hilariously caught in the image of the Moody car, which was kept from crashing with its occupants into the ravine by one of Uncle Nathan's religious signs—"Destruction Is At Hand"! There it remains throughout most of the novel impossibly suspended on Banner Top—its motor running, its tires exploding, its precarious equilibrium depending on an amiable simpleton in the back seat—waiting to be saved. And it is. The salvation is not exactly the kind Nathan had in mind, but it is the kind of salvation that occurs in the world of *Losing Battles*: it's a bit battered but it'll run.

Much the same impulse, though in this instance tonally quite different, occurs in the very brief night scene, which is the literal and symbolic dark time of the novel. Granny, anguished by the end of the reunion, pleads with Vaughn, neither knowing nor caring who he is, to get into bed with her. And Miss Beulah lying in bed says to her husband, "I've got it to stand and I've got to stand it. And you've got to stand it. . . . After they've all gone home, Ralph, and the children's in bed, that's what's left. Standing it." Although Welty allows her characters their nocturnal loneliness, she does not allow the scene to be taken over by it. After all, another day is coming. Describing Vaughn's ride through the moonlight, Welty, in one of the rare times when she speaks in her own voice, comments, "Even after people gave up each other's company, said goodby and went home, if there was only one left, Vaughn Renfro, the world around him was still one huge, soul-defying reunion." And the night scene significantly ends with Miss Beulah rushing onto the porch to snatch up her granddaughter, Lady May, and carry her back to her own bed "as if a life had been saved."

Generally speaking, critics have been reluctant to give full assent to the novel's "wholly affirmative" comic vision. As I have indicated, the tendency has been to darken the novel, this darkening coming in various shades. It has been characterized as "elegiac," as another Welty treatment of "the illusions with which people protect themselves in the losing battles of their experience," as a story of "the separateness of each of us isolated within our shells of individuality." But nowhere is this inclination more apparent than in an interview with Eudora Welty conducted by Charles T. Bunting for the *Southern Review*. When he remarked that "Miss Julia Mortimer has, of course, lost her battle to educate the Renfros, but really it's a losing battle for everybody in the novel, isn't it?" Welty gently but firmly disagreed: "I wanted to show indomitability there. I don't feel it's a novel of despair at all. I feel it's more a novel of admiration for the human being who can cope with any condition, even ignorance, and keep a courage, a joy of life, even, that is unquenchable. But I see human beings as *valuable*. Each life is very valuable in itself, regardless, and in spite of everything." And in the *Jackson Daily News* (5 April 1970), she characterized her novel as being "about all the battles which we *seem* to be losing." The operative word here is the one I have italicized.

One should note in these remarks that Welty's "admiration" is not selective: it apparently applies to *both* sides of the "battle"—Julia Mortimer and the Renfro/Beecham family. Welty loves all of her characters (Cleo perhaps excepted) and, as Jack says, "You can't blame who you love." This love, which comes of the author's "generous dispensation of the understanding," manifests itself primarily as "an angelic ingenuity" in the way of narrative—an almost magical balancing of all the elements in the novel. In contrast to such grand impartiality, the critics of the novel have tended to take sides, to give their allegiance (albeit some with agreeable qualifications) to the "anti-family" forces—Miss Mortimer and all those (like Gloria) who fight against what has been variously characterized as the suffocating insularity, pettiness, smug ignorance, and prejudice of the back country family. This negative response is at least partly the result, I believe, of two separate but related things: the ease with which the reader can identify the greatness in Julia and the powerfully concentrated accounts we are given of her suffering in the service of that greatness; and the ease with which we can miss, or at least slight, the sufferings of the family because they come to us either in a ritualized form which deliberately deflects the pain or in an almost offhand and glancing manner.

Julia's losing battles are so overpowering because they are so painfully concentrated in Lexie's account of her last days and in Julia's final letter to the world. Early in the novel when Gloria has torn her knee protecting Lady May from the Buick, Etoyle says to her, "I'm on your side now, Gloria.

. . . Know why? Because you're the one that's bleeding." Precisely: we can *see* Julia bleeding. A mind watching itself going back on itself; the desperate attempt to hold onto some vestige of what she has given her life for, if only symbolically, like the speller she sleeps on; the waiting for ex-students who never come; her summation, without self-pity, of her failure to transform the community; her refusal to quit fighting even though she knows she's just about licked—"I'm ready for all they send me"; her lonely death on the road, her last words—"What was the trip for?"—shadowed with the ultimate doubt. It could, indeed, as the judge says, "make a stone cry."

That the family's sufferings might not make a stone cry is hardly the sign of their lack of human cost—that has been enormous. It is rather the index of the family's capacity for absorbing private anguish into its communal life, of which the reunion is the annual rite. They have not come together for lamentation, so what we do learn of their griefs is either undramatically imbedded in their "history" or comes to us in scattered fragments, often impelled against their inclinations by such circumstances as Cleo's vulgar prying or the puzzle of Gloria's parentage. It is harder to be on their side because it is harder to *see* them bleeding.

The family has nothing; they inhabit, as Welty put it in the *Paris Review*, "a bare stage." The Renfro store was easy prey for a sharpshooter like Dearman; the farm, mortgaged acres of clay on which it rains too much or not at all, can no longer raise enough for them to eat; with Jack in jail, they have had to trade the horse for food "to keep us alive" and the beloved truck for pride—to put up a new roof which will say that they have not gone under yet. Life has been, as Beck quietly puts it, "a lot of doing without." If they speak of their material deprivations laconically, it is not because they can't, like the inhabitants of some Tobacco Road, feel them. One passage—the only one like it in the novel—points to feelings that go deeper than the words they choose for them. "Cleo," Noah remembers, "the old place here was plum stocked with squirrel when we was boys. It was overrun with quail. And if you never saw the deer running in here, I saw 'em. It was filled—it was filled!—with every kind of good thing, this old dwelling, when me and the rest of us Beecham boys grew up here. . . ."

The downward path to government handouts is in some ways the least of what they suffer. There are more grievous hurts, of which Nathan's cutting off of his offending hand for his double murder is both the most obvious and the most terrible. The seven Beecham children have not only early lost their parents by drowning, but have had to face the awful possibility that their mother and father were running away from *them*. Beneath Noah's raucous, life-loving hilarity there is a rod of iron guilt: he has always blamed himself for his parents' death because he was in the road, having intuited the disaster, when they rode off into the night, but couldn't stop them. Significantly, it is the only family story he has shared with his new wife before she comes to the reunion. Beneath Beulah's powerful and commanding presence is similar anguish: she has lived with the belief that she is responsible for the emasculation of her brother Sam Dale, the darling of the family in her generation as Jack is the darling in his. For those brief moments that the family entertains the possibility that Sam Dale is Gloria's father, the intensity of Beulah's secret hurt breaks out into the open. With the exultatioin born of exquisite relief, Beulah cries out, "Gloria's here, and she's proof, living proof! I didn't do hurt to my own, after all. I can die happy! Can't I?" Only gradually do we learn what lies beneath Nanny's jolly obesity, why she can't keep loving hands off any child that passes her, why any talk of children evokes a bemusement that approaches the tragic. Her mother gave her away when she was a baby, and all she has ever had of motherhood are what lies beneath those two small stones in the cemetery "bearing the same one word, 'Infant.' " Beck and Curtis have had nine sons but they're all gone. "All nine!" twice in the novel Curtis murmurs with appalled disbelief, "and they're never coming home." Mr. Renfro, a man so gentle and modest that he "bows to the day," has been a lifelong cripple from an accident he suffered shortly before his marriage. He carries his twisted body as if apologizing for the fact that he has not ever been able to do a whole man's work on the farm. And his sister Lexie's hardness of manner only imperfectly hides the disappointment that she was too unattractive ever to be a wife and too dumb to learn Virgil so that she could become a teacher.

The sufferings of the family have been formidable, although to bunch them up as I have done gives them an intensity they are not meant to have in the reading of the novel. But it is necessary to acknowledge them in order to keep the family and therefore the novel in perspective. When Julia says that "there's a measure of enjoyment" in having spent a lifetime in what she considers a losing battle, we assent to the affirmation because we know the conditions out of which that modulated affirmation has been won. The same should be true of the family. In response to Gloria's self-dramatizing remark that she was having a baby "and you can die from that," Beulah, speaking for the family, wryly replies, "You can die from anything if you try good and hard." I have tried to indicate what gives such a remark authority.

If, however, only Julia and her "losing battles" are taken as normative, then inevitably "the other side," those (in her words) "who held the fort" against the learning and rational intelligence she championed, becomes the negative force in the novel. Such a view, as I will try to show, distorts the comic design of the novel, the "continuous attainment of balance."

First of all, as others have noted, Julia is a marvelous woman who is a teacher of fierce dedication, not (thankfully) another saintly schoolmarm. The will, energy, and sacrifice she expended in the service of teaching her pupils are only to be admired, especially since much of what we learn of her as a teacher comes from the mouths of those who consider her zeal to have been their "bane." Her kindness to the sick and rejected Rachael Sojourner, whom she taught to sew when she realized the girl could not do "mental arithmetic," and to Willy Trimble, whom she taught to do carpentry when she realized that he could not learn academic subjects, reveals a woman of both sense and sensibility, not some kind of teaching machine; so too does her hauling a ten-gallon can of milk to school each day and her teaching the kids to swim because at times the Bywy River got high enough to drown in. Her handsomeness—in her youth she was the best-looking woman around—reminds us that she chose her life by conviction not default. And in her letter to Judge Moody we see a fine mind groping honestly and painfully toward some kind of understanding and wisdom. But, it should be stressed, what is grand about Miss Julia Mortimer, teacher, belongs to her and not to her profession. This is a necessary distinction because the novel does not authorize the wholesale elevation of Education over what has been learned in the way of the reunion, what in the *Paris Review* Eudora Welty has called, "a narrative sense of human destiny": "They learn and teach and think and enjoy that way." The other teachers we meet, those riding in the church bus to Julia's funeral, are not a particularly attractive lot. "Isn't it the luckiest thing it's a Sunday she picked?" one of them says. "Suppose it had been a school day, like tomorrow. We'd been cooped up." Hardly bearers of what Gloria calls "the torch" of learning. And by no stretch of the imagination could anything we know of Gloria lead us to believe that had she not become Mrs. Jack Renfro she would have been another Miss Mortimer. That she once entertained the idea that she would eventually outshine her mentor is the index of her naiveté, of her rather aggressive over-evaluation of herself. Finally, it should be recalled, the most grievous error in judgment belongs to Judge Moody, who, because he does not understand the amiably antagonistic game that Jack and Curly play ("never got it through his head what it was all about"), sends Jack to jail as "a lesson to the rest" that there must be respect for the law and for those who have been "raised to office." Considering the real situation, the principle is absurdly misapplied.

Julia Mortimer has been, until nearly the very end of her life, a romantic empiricist (her letter to Moody, as Gloria disapprovingly recognizes, exhibits "a change"); it is what has given shape and meaning to her existence and has been the source of many of the fine things she has done with her life. She had a rationalistic program for the improvement of society—"She wanted everything brought out in the wide open, to see and be known"—and had no doubt that if you firmly pointed out to people what was expected of them—progress—they would "measure up." She believes that any question rationally framed (such as who is Gloria's father) can be rationally answered by "a good brain." "She said every mystery had its right answer—we just had to find it. That's what mysteries were given to us for."

The comic side of Julia's character emerges from the odd, even irrational, twists her passionate convictions are made to take—teaching in a cyclone; telling Gloria that all she (Julia) needs to know to decide if a boy is right for Gloria is "his name and age and the year I taught him"; rejecting Jack as a husband for Gloria because he received only two-thirds of a point over 75, "And 75 is passing"; demanding that she be buried under the schoolhouse. As for her belief that every mystery can be solved, the novel demurs. The identity of Gloria's father is never established; what Mamma and Papa Beecham were doing when they rode off in the middle of the night remains forever "something between man and wife . . . and it's what no other soul would have no way of knowing"; exactly why Nathan killed Dearman is never explained; "lost's lost." Julia's last spoken words on earth—"what was the trip for?"—are repeated by the first words of Lady May's life—"What you huntin', man?" Two forms of one question, to which there is no answer given, save, perhaps, one which begs it: the trip is for the trip, life is for the living of it.

The balanced characterization of Julia is important to the novel's comic poise. But more important is the true fate of "what happened to what she was." Julia (mostly) considers her life to have been a failure, "except in those cases that you can count off on your fingers." The text, however, does not support such a sad summation. Julia has won more than she and "the other side" realize. I do not mean here simply the barefoot boys she prodded into becoming professors, physicians, lawyers and clergymen or the fact that "all Alliance, half of Ludlow, and most of Foxtown" attend her funeral. I mean what she "won" in the camp of her presumptive enemies in the battle, the Beechman/Renfro clan. Perhaps Julia herself, at the end, had an inkling of such a possibility when she wrote that "when the battle's over, something may dawn there—with no help from the teacher, no help from the pupil, no help from the book."

On several occasions Miss Beulah remarks with exasperation that Julia's funeral has become a part of the reunion. It has indeed. (The reverse is also true: the reunion has become a part of the funeral.) Resist as it may, the reunion is nevertheless forced to listen to an account of Julia's last days, to hear her last will and testament read to them, and to have to accept the incredible news that Julia will be buried not under her beloved schoolhouse but in their sacrosanct burial ground. This last fact is not, however, merely an unexpected comic reversal, though it is that too; it is, rather, a symbolically apt finale to what has not been much noted—that Julia is to be buried with those whom she has deeply touched in all the days of their lives. It turns out to be one of Welty's angelic ingenuities that the battle between the family and Julia Mortimer, like Jack and Curly's fistfights or the family's sworn enmity towards Judge Moody, is not the collision of discrete antagonisms but, paradoxically, of "foes well-matched or sweethearts come together." The novel suggests that the relationship between Julia and the family, as with all the other relationships in the novel, is that of interpenetrating polarities, foes *and* sweethearts; only the "foes" has been emphasized, however, to the detriment of Welty's extraordinary balancing act.

First of all, the family is not a univocal chorus. Different voices speak differently and even the same voice does not always sound the same. Certainly the strophe (so to speak) of the family "ode" sounds the note of hostility—carping, perverse, even mean-spirited; and in Lexie's account of her battle with Julia in the last days of the teacher's life, apparently something worse.

"Yes'm," says Dolphus, "she taught the generations. She was our cross to bear." For Nanny and Birdie, too, Julia's obsessive commitment to learning—"She'd follow you, right to your door"—took the joy out of childhood for "the poor little children." "She put an end to good fishing" says it all. Some of them take a curious pleasure in their successful resistance to learning, perversely proud that Julia didn't penetrate their "pore hot skulls." "It was so far fetched," says Birdie, [but] "I've gone a long ways ahead of it now!" Yet Percy, without outrageous unreason, complains that Julia didn't make them "*stay* in school, and learn some profit." Like any self-satisfied ignoramus, some of them dismiss what they do not know as not worth knowing and those who know it as not worth emulating. She expected too much out of people and "never did learn to please"; she was a cracked old maid driven slightly batty by devoting herself to accumulating books rather than children. How else, they ask, can one explain a grown healthy woman reading in the afternoon, throwing herself on the dictionary during the cyclone, spending all she had on a library, and wasting her lovely voice on poems, multiplication tables and other such "rigmarole."

These moral vulgarities (as Julia herself finally realizes) are the result of the family's deep-seated and passionate commitment to surviving in the only way it knows how: "we've all just tried to last as long as we can by just sticking together," Beulah says. Julia's assault on that value—"She wanted us to quit worshipping ourselves so wholehearted"—is both an unbearable insult and a powerful threat aimed at the very nerve center of the family's life. So they fight back in the only way they know how, and it disfigures them. How marring "the desperation of staying alive against all odds" can become is, symbolically speaking, revealed in the family's climactic rejection of what Julia stood for—Lexie's refusal to give the dying Julia a pencil to write with or a book to read.

The "antistrophe," which takes various forms, both actual and symbolic, is, I believe, more decisive, thus justifying, as I've already indicated, the site where Welty has Julia finally laid to rest—with the family. Side by side with the criticisms of Julia, but almost never offered as literal response to them, are quite different views of Julia as teacher and human being. Curtis, for example, recalls Julia as someone who "was ready to teach herself to death for you. . . . Whether you wanted her to or not didn't make any difference. But my suspicion was she did want you to *deserve* it" (p. 240). Beck, with "awe and compassion" in her voice, says that Julia "put a little more of her own heart" into teaching than she even knew, which is why she went at it "just as hard as a steam engine." Lexie plays homage to Julia's vision in her recollection of the teacher's first words to Banner School— "Nothing in this world can measure up to the joy you'll bring me if you allow me to teach you something." Most surprising of all is Beulah. As the novel's most vociferous defender of the value of "the splendid mothers at home," she is apparently Julia's chief antagonist, and has been accused of viewing Julia "with unreasoning hatred." Yet she confesses, in an unguarded moment, that Julia is "responsible for a good deal I know right here today," and has evidently accepted with equanimity her daughter Elvie's ambition to follow in the teacher's footsteps—"A fine way to get to be a teacher," she tells the child when Elvie expresses a preference for attending the rescue of the Buick rather than school.

Beulah's actual if unperceived congruence with Julia, the coming together of foes as sweethearts, is delicately reinforced and amplified by a symbolic pattern involving spelling. Julia's great public triumph, it will be recalled, was when her Banner pupils spelled down the Mississippi legislature. But for the family, spelling would seem to be just another kind of "farfetched" memory work, the use of which escapes them. Yet when Willy Trimble produces the speller which lay under Julia's pillow, Beulah instinctively reaches out to take it in her hands; and then suddenly, as if remembering what she is supposed to feel, thrusts it back. But the contact has been made, and it evokes for Beulah the precious memory of her own public triumph—the day she spelled the school down "like a row of tin soldiers," so excited that she wet her britches. The full implications of this convergence at the speller emerge in the figure of Vaughn, Jack's younger brother, about whom until the night scene we know little more than that "He'll never be Jack" and that he is presently the best speller in his class. The scene in which Vaughn, "moonlit," rides the mule through the night to pull the school bus from the ditch is stylistically unlike any other part of the novel; the prose is reminiscent of, for example, "First Love"—mysterious, evocative, resistant to paraphrase, as if it were a projection of and a tribute to a sensibility still mute. The reason this change occurs is revealed when we discover that Vaughn loves school with a passion that is almost pain and watch him with the new geography book he traded out of Curly Stovall: "He dragged it to his cheek, where he could smell its print, sharper, blacker, dearer than the smell of new shoes." The last time we see him tells us where he is going. Clutching his school books to his side, he leaps towards the new teacher he "was so ready to worship" and lands almost in her arms. He has, in effect, landed in the arms of Miss Julia. "When the battle's over, something may dawn there—with no help from the teacher, no help from the pupil."

Julia not only moves forward through Beulah to Vaughn but backward to the family's beginnings. Early in the novel the family, out of love and need, "bring" Jack out of Parchman to the reunion. In a sense, it has also "brought" Julia. Banner School, we learn, is a creation of the family. Lexie and Ralph Renfro's grandfather believed it was "something they ought to have" (" 'Never dreamed that!' Aunt Nanny cried") and, after a generation, "Miss Julia Mortimer was the living answer to Old Preacher Renfro's prayer" (" 'I never knew that either!' cried Uncle Noah Webster").

What the family proclaims it has learned from the emergence of Julia into their lives is the meaning of the Islamic proverb—Beware of answered prayers! What it does not know, or resists acknowledging, is how deeply Julia is implicated in their personal history. Granny, for example, brings a puzzled hush to the reunion when she recalls how when Julia lived with the family "she and I could set and catch our breath when the day's over, and confab a little about the state the world was in." "But all that happened a mighty long time ago," Birdie objects in an attempt to push back the implications of the image. To which Beck significantly replies, "Feelings don't get old! . . . We do, but they don't. They go on." It is, however, in the relationship between Julia and Nathan, the family's darkest figure, that we can feel how deeply and decisively the souls of Julia and the family are intertwined. No one in the world knows, except some of the family and Julia, to whom he has confessed, that Nathan killed Dearman and allowed an innocent Negro to hang for his crime. His poor wayfaring stranger's life, that he has any life at all, he owes to Julia. "Nathan," she so beautifully told him when he was lost, "even when there's nothing left to hope for, you can start again from there, and go your way and *be good*." Once a year he returns to the only things that he allows to sweeten his self-imposed asceticism: the reunion of the family and "breakfast-time visits" with Julia. And he wanders the world with the memory of the only things he loves—his family *and* Julia. He breaks his silence in the novel with "Many a little schoolhouse I pass on the mountainside today is a sister to Banner, and I pass it wondering if I was to knock on the door wouldn't she come running out, all unchanged."

Just as the force of Julia-as-teacher moves with increasing momentum from the early Renfros through Beulah to culminate in Vaughn, so too does Julia as a moral presence move from Granny through Nathan to Jack. In his long day's living, Jack has been both pulled by the family reunion and pushed to the funeral of Miss Julia Mortimer. Only the uncomprehending figures at the funeral think he has no business being there. Although he has "never laid eyes" on Julia, Jack, in a translucent moment of imaginative sympathy, comes to "love her" because, as he explains to an astonished Gloria, "I heard her story."

Julia, then, willy-nilly, continues to exert an almost mythic force on the lives of the family. They dismiss as absurd Cleo's suggestion that she knew "one like her"; for them there has been and could only be one Julia. Whatever stance toward Julia they try to take, the irreducible fact is that she is *there*, as much (or almost as much) a part of their "story" as their "feeling of the solidity of the family," which Eudora Welty characterized in the *Southern Review* as "the strongest thing in the book." Miss Beulah, "with some darkness" in her voice, says, "the littler you wish to see of some people, the plainer you may come to remember 'em. . . . Even against your will. I can't tell you why, so don't ask me. But I can see that old school teacher this minute plainer than I can see you, Lexie Renfro, after your back is turned."

The suggestion that the true relationship between the family and Julia is one of unconscious congruities, interacting polarities, unperceived affinities as well as moral antipodes meets its severest test in the figure of Lexie. Her treatment of Julia in the last days of Julia's life has been called sadistic; and she has been accused of taking a perversely cruel pleasure in recounting that treatment.

Lexie is the hardest member of the family, the least gracious. Her tough-old-bird personality is, there is ample reason to believe, her way of having maintained some dignity in the face of a life in which she lives nowhere and has suffered the double blow of being wanted as neither wife nor teacher. It's her way, as she puts it, "of being equal to circumstances." Her home is where she takes care of those too sick and old to take care of themselves; everything she has in the world she carries in a single bag. She comes to Julia when the teacher, against her will and to her surprise, has been "put out to pasture," and when old age has worn down Julia's body and intensified her characteristic indifference to pleasing into an aggressive hostility. Julia drove everybody away, Lexie says, and "then she wondered what had happened to everybody." Having no other object, Julia's bitterness turns on Lexie, whom she strikes, calls fool and old woman (though Lexie is eleven years younger), and insults: "Suppose you take your presence out of here. How can I read with you in the house with me?" "You get out of my house, old woman. Go home! If you've got a home"—a cruelly aimed barb.

Lexie fights back: "I reckon what it amounted to was the two of us settling down finally to see which would be the first to wear the other one out." Lexie ties Julia in bed to keep her from running off and hurting herself; refuses her a pencil when she sees that Julia's letters are attacks on people ("Listen, Julia. If you've got something this bad to say about human nature, . . . why don't you go ahead and send it to the President of the United States? What do you want to waste it on us for?", though she does mail them; and meanly refuses to bring Julia a book because Julia doesn't name a specific title. In coming to the runion, Lexie, it turns out, has left Julia alone to die.

It is important to remember, however, that of all the family Lexie has most loved Julia. "I worshipped her! Worshipped Miss Julia Mortimer!" she suddenly declares. She cried when Julia, her "inspiration," moved from the Renfros to the Vaughns. When Lexie was a child, Julia "encouraged" her to be a teacher, made the little girl feel important, worthwhile. But "the ones that think highly of you," Lexie remarks, "they change, or leave you behind, get married, flit, go crazy—." When Julia beat at Lexie, Lexie asked her, "Why don't you quit fighting kind hands? . . . I *love you*." To which Julia replied, "Only way to keep myself alive!" The answer might serve Lexie too, but it doesn't. Though it is deeply embedded in the rough bluntness of her telling, Lexie is grieving at what she has done. When Beulah, who has tried to cut short the story at several points, says that she hopes that Lexie is now "satisfied" since she got to tell the whole story, Lexie replies, "You don't get over it all that quick—what some of 'em make you do." So far from being motivated by cruel pleasure, Lexie tells the story out of a troubling guilt. Her story of Julia begins in shame and pain and ends in conversion. Suddenly, over one hundred pages later, Lexie, glaring defiantly at the reunion, announces that she knows now how to treat Mr. Hugg, to whose house she is going: "It's to give him every single thing he wants. Everything Mr. Hugg asks for—give it to him." Once again Julia has touched a member of the clan.

The relationship between Julia and the family is only one, though the most important, relationship in the novel in which oppositions turn out to be "like foes well-matched or sweethearts come together," in which collisions are both hurts and comminglings. Jack and Curly Stovall have fought with each other all their lives. Jack is "the sweetest and hardest-working boy . . . in all Creation," who can't blame anyone alive and loves everything from little birds and dead snakes to people; Curly, the spiritual descendant of Dearman, is a goatish "greedy hog," one of those who would take the joy out of life. But when Jack returns from the jail to which Curly helped send him, they embrace each other in a transport of cordiality. And at the end of the novel we learn that Ella Fay is going to marry Curly and so make him, like it or not, a part of the family. The reunion talks a good game of hating Moody "the Booger") for sending their beloved Jack to jail—"Just let Moody dare to come up in my yard!"—but when he does, what they do is to feed him, treat him with kindness and consideration, give him and his wife the best sleeping accommodations, and rescue his Buick. Mr. Renfro especially takes "a shine to the fellow. . . . I couldn't tell you why. . . . I just did, that's all. If he'd stay a week, I'd take him turkey hunting." Jack must pay back Moody for sending him to jail. Moody, unknowingly, facilitates Jack's escape when Jack rides the back of his car part of the way home from Parchman. But when Moody's car goes into a ditch, Jack, not knowing who he is, pushes it out. When he learns he has helped his enemy, Jack sets out to get Moody into another ditch. But when Moody swerves to avoid hitting Gloria and Lady May and lands his car on Banner Top, Jack sets out to save the Buick. The almost magical way in which disparates are made to link—like the hilarious "chain" of people, animals, and machines which effects the car's rescue—is perfectly caught in the final moment between the family's darling and its villain: "Judge Moody put out his rope-burned hand, Jack put up his bloody one, and they shook." Ultimately, then, in the comic world of *Losing Battles* there are no "sides," though people take them. Like the election posters nailed to trees, "There were the faces of losers and winners, the forgotten and remembered, still there together and looking like members of the same family."

Comedy must make us feel, if for no longer than the enchanted time of reading, that Death and all those little deaths which are its harbingers have been triumphed over. It can do this, speaking largely, by the use of luck, wit, or as in the case of *The Tempest*, literal magic. Welty uses none of these, though her novel is closer to the feel of *The Tempest*; but her magic is the kind that can be assimilated into the texture of a realistic novel. Julia in the family plot and the reunion at the funeral; Jack and Moody clasping hands; sour Lexie sweetly off to give Mr. Hugg everything he wants; awful Curly a member of the family; Gloria, the devotée of Being Nobody But Herself, to have (lucky for her) family "piled" all over her; Grandpa Vaughn traded for Lady May; the Buick, like the people, beating the laws of probability, mechanics, and gravity. Destruction Is At Hand!? Hardly. "There's room for everything, and time for everybody, if you take your day the way it comes along and try not to be much later than you can help." The glory of *Losing Battles* is that it allows you to feel what it would be like *really* to believe in life.

MICHAEL KREYLING

The Robber Bridegroom
and the Pastoral Dream

Following [Alfred] Kazin's lead, I want to consider *The Robber Bridegroom* in the company of other versions of American pastoral laced with irony. But I also want to emphasize that its unity arises primarily from within, in artistic choices often taken for granted; in images, character, and symbolic action.

I realize here that I run the risk of overanalysis, of explaining the jokes. Indeed, in *The Robber Bridegroom* the sustaining power of the humor—of which a few examples follow—cannot be overstated. Rosamond, the damsel of the tale, suffers the humiliation of being robbed of every stitch by a dashing bandit. Is she flustered? Not for a second; she calmly returns home clothed only in her tresses and a straight face. Her stepmother demands to know the whereabouts of the herbs she had sent the feckless girl to gather in her apron. What herbs? What apron? "In God's name," cries Rosamond's father, "the child is naked as a jay bird."

In another instance, the hapless gnome of the story, Goat (an apt name, for he not only has to butt his way into and out of things, he is also the "goat" of Salome's foiled revenge plot against Rosamond), comes upon Rosamond weeping in the tent of her Indian captors:

"Good evening, why are you crying?"

"Oh, I have lost my husband, and he has lost me, and we are both tied up to be killed in the morning," she cried.

Sometimes damsels are more aggravation than they are worth.

"Then cry on," said Goat, "for I never expect to hear a better reason."

And Rosamond, thoroughly pregnant with the hero's twins, has taken to the road to find Jamie, their father. She encounters Mike Fink, who has

From *Eudora Welty's Achievement of Order.* © 1980 by Louisiana State University Press.

been exiled from the river for losing face to Jamie Lockhart in a fight. Fink, convinced that he has murdered Jamie, is just as sure that Jamie is a ghost come back to haunt him. Rosamond knows otherwise and tells Fink to notify said ghost, at his next materialization, that he is soon to be a father. "Oh," Fink said. "Ghosts are getting more powerful every day in these parts."

The wry, deadpan tone with which Welty retells the legendary tale of the Natchez frontier propels the novella. In fact, the caricatures may be taken for the whole meaning of *The Robber Bridegroom*. Alfred Uhry, who has written book and lyrics for a musical adaptation of the novella, emphasizes this aspect. He has chosen to omit both the Indians and the serious aspects of Clement's character.

If jokes were all *The Robber Bridegroom* relied upon, then Trilling's objection on the grounds of simplicity could be readily allowed. But the novella is not limited, in its technique, just to the jokes; it reaches for something beyond the momentary relief of laughter. One laughs at Clement Musgrove much differently from the way one laughs at his silly daughter, her slightly ridiculous hero, her lavishly evil stepmother, or any of the menagerie of eccentrics who appear in the brief story. Clement is foolish in the way that Don Quixote is foolish. One laughs at them both with full sympathy; for the cruel, absurd, treacherous world they wrestle with in innocent vanity can never be subdued. Nor can they happily live in the world of "ponderous realities" and "practicable schemes."

Besides Clement, the Indians spark something other than laughter. They are recreated with a depth and quality of sympathy sometimes found in Cooper. Not the whooping stereotypes of greasepaint westerns, they have nobility, mystery, beauty, and pride. They are the spirit of the country. Clement and the Indians furnish a certain gravity in this light-hearted tale.

Welty's choice of a real place for her "fairy tale" infuses it with the undercurrent of irony and deliberate seriousness in which the Indians and Clement move. Of this river country setting Welty has written, "Whatever is significant and whatever is tragic in a place live as long as the place does, though they are unseen, and the new life will be built upon those things— regardless of commerce and the way of rivers and roads and other vagrancies."

Rodney, Mississippi, teems with this unseen life. It began its history as a thriving town on the Mississippi River. Delta cotton went to market through its port. Clement Musgrove's crop goes out to the New Orleans market through Rodney; he and his money return through it to begin the story. Sometime after the Civil War, however, the river was to alter its course and leave Rodney a ghost town. In the novella, that doom hovers in Rodney's future, shading the high jinks with a sentence of death. The place in which *The Robber Bridegroom* happens is both real and imaginary, the timeless land of legend and the changing world of real historical and geographical events. Rodney is a ghost, symbolically cut adrift when time and the river went away and left it.

Rodney is not the only ghost whose presence tempers the novella with seriousness. The Indians, who appear at the opening and close of the story and whom all the white pioneers fear as they fear the dark, encircling wilderness itself, are both real and ghostly.

The Indians of *The Robber Bridegroom*, although their tribe is never named, are modeled on the Natchez Indians. The Natchez had been wiped out years before the imagined events of the novella. Yet the facts of their demise ring significantly in the undercurrent of the story. They had been massacred in retaliation for a massacre of their own, and the remnants of the tribe were sold into slavery in Santo Domingo by the French. Besides their name, they left behind the vivid memory of their distinctiveness.

> It is not strange to think that a unique nation among Indians lived in this beautiful country. The origin of the Natchez is still in mystery. But their people, five villages in the seventeenth century, were unique in this country and they were envied by the other younger nations—the Choctaws helped the French in their final dissolution. In Mississippi they were remnants surely of medievalism. They were proud and cruel, gentle-mannered and ironic, handsome, extremely tall, intellectual, elegant, pacific, and ruthless. Fire, death, sacrifice formed the spirit of the Natchez' worship. They did not now, however, make war.
>
> ("Some Notes on River Country")

The Natchez, in a way the incarnate spirit of the natural place, fell, as the place itself also fell, before the advancing waves of civilization. Their residual spirit and the echoes of a thriving Rodney haunt the tale, not with a haunting so "mundane as a ghost," but with questions much more solemn than those of happy endings.

Through Rodney and the Natchez; Welty keeps us aware that no matter what possibilities of wealth and empire the future may seem to offer, human time is finite; and nothing man builds or accumulates is permanent against time. The Indians are in the throes of change and extinction; Rodney is a static omen of the same impending change. The Indians' way of life and its passing dramatize the meaning of change; the presence of Rodney bodes it.

Change is not necessarily progress; here it seems to be loss. The Indians inhabit the enchanted forest of the novella in a mysterious way that contrasts sharply with the noisy intrusion of the pioneers. The distinction creates the theme of oblivion haunting the works of man, for every step the white pioneers confidently take is shadowed by the unseen, doomed Indians, whose harmonious relationship with the forest is coming to an end. The Indians enjoy an organic union with the place, appearing and dissolving in the surrounding forest, to the eyes of the pioneers, as if Indian nature were not restricted merely to the human but partook of the animal and the vegetable as well. White men never spy the Indians first; they see them only after the Indians have chosen to be seen, when escape from a "reckoning" is impossible. Clement Musgrove's memory of his first captivity by the Indians expresses his pioneer astonishment at the Indians' mysterious presence in the surrounding wilderness. "They showed their pleasure and their lack of surprise well enough, when we climbed and crept up to them as they waited on all fours, disguised in their bearskins and looking as far as they could look, out from the head of the bluff."

The cunning art of disguise links the Indians intimately with their natural place. And the lack of it accentuates the pioneers' estrangement from nature. Beyond the closed circle of their immediate, well-lighted camp, the pioneers enter an unknown universe. In their fears, the Indians are always lurking just beyond what can be clearly seen and controlled. The image of the encircling Indians suggests all that the settlers fear—suffering, death, the unknown. The Indians, then, must be eradicated.

The Robber Bridegroom, although a "fairy tale," an enchanted story, acknowledges the torture, death, and violence that the Indians inflict on the pioneers, and vice versa. This bloody violence was noted by John Peale Bishop in his review of the novella, but he could not decide what part it was meant to play. The theme of extinction and change did not fully occur to him. Extinction and the fear of it are as much a part of *The Robber Bridegroom* as the cartoons, the borrowings from Grimm, and the frontier folklore. In this theme, violence as an indispensable part of the pioneering enterprise plays an essential part. *The Robber Bridegroom* is properly a "local legend," which "has a personal immediacy, a cruelty, and a directness glossed over in the fairy tale." Beautiful though it was, Rodney was founded on violence. The Indians resisted invasion violently and were crushed. This is the contradiction that maims the pastoral ideal, that cooled Coverdale's enthusiasm for Blithedale, that lay behind Gatsby's "incorruptible dream." The means corrupt the end; he who acquiesces in the end, acquiesces in the means.

Our glimpse of the Indians while they are yet in their full pride, on the peak from which they will be pushed by civilization, comes from Clement's early life history, which he relates to Jamie Lockhart in the Rodney Inn.

Clement remembers the Indians as both gay and cruel. But, as Jamie comments, "This must have been long ago. . . . For they are not so fine now, and cannot do so much to prisoners as that." The Indians had struck Clement with their imperiousness and fierce pride. They were supreme in their power over their captives. He remembers: "We had to go whirling and dizzied in a dance we had never suspected lay in our limbs. We had to be humiliated and tortured and enjoyed, and finally, with most precise formality, to be decreed upon. All of them put on their blazing feathers and stood looking us down as if we were little mice." Then with scorn the Indians put to death Clement's infant son, and with contempt dismissed him into the wilderness with his daughter Rosamond and future wife Salome.

The Indians had full control. Their realm was unfenced, unsurveyed, undivided. The onslaught of pioneers was but a trickle and well within the Indians' power to intercept. In the first "reckoning" episode of the novella, the Indians do decree and pronounce. The time is still their own.

Nevertheless, extinction is their fate. If Jamie Lockhart, the successful bandit and gentleman, has his way, the Indians will be eradicated as if they were ants at his picnic: "The savages are so clever they are liable to last out, no matter how we stamp upon them." Clement, however, is not so vehement; vengeance does not consume him, even though he, not Jamie, has lost loved ones at the hands of the Indians. Clement contemplates the Indians' fate with a puzzled melancholy. His melancholy springs from the moment of mutual recognition when the Indians turned him out into the wilderness bound to Salome. In that moment a "mark" was fixed on Clement. "There is nothing that you can see," he tells Jamie, "but something came out of their eyes." Clement cannot say what his mark means; but he feels that he shares the Indians' strange and doomed relationship with time: "They are sure of the future growing smaller always."

The future is also dwindling for the two men, the robber and the planter, as they sit and talk in the tavern. The town itself will eventually be removed from the mainstream. Although the Indians and the town of Rodney may be seen as symbols for limited time, extinction, the vanity of human pride and industry, they are never explicitly identified by the author as her symbols. Their meaning would be impaired by direct identification. Welty uses place more subtly, trusting it to generate its own symbolic meaning in its own time: "Place in fiction is the named, identified, concrete, exact and exacting, and therefore credible, gathering-spot of all that has been felt, is about to be experienced, in the novel's progress." The extinction of the Natchez and the eventual death of Rodney are always "about to be experienced"; they haunt the place of this novella. Welty's choice of place is essential to the meaning of *The Robber Bridegroom* and must be understood to appreciate her technique. It is not the case, as Chester Eisinger has written, that "the accuracy of historical detail constitutes an act of harmless piety."

With the passing of the Indians, an intimate human connection with the natural world passes too. They are so closely united with the world of animals and forest that disguise, as Clement can testify, is as natural to them as their own skin. Beyond the lights and noise of the artificial world of the pioneers, the Indians are always watching, ready to proclaim a "reckoning." When the second and climactic reckoning falls due, the Indians materialize and apprehend the white offenders as if they (the Indians) were the avenging shapes of the forest itself. The bush at Salome's side "comes alive," and she is taken; a "red hand" materializes in an apparently empty forest, and Clement is taken; an Indian suddenly appears before Rosamond "in the mask of a spotty leopard," and she is carried off.

The Indians seize the captives to avenge their people's rape and desecration, symbolically committed by Little Harp, the vicious killer of the Natchez Trace, who violated and killed an innocent Indian girl while Jamie's robber cohorts cheered. This violation scene is a departure from the fantasy of the fairy tale and a vivid example of the violence that threads through the story as local legend. There is not the least sliver of irony in the scene. On a table littered with the leavings of a meal, Little Harp first cuts off the drugged girl's finger, then throws himself upon her. When he leaves her, she is dead; no magic wand can revive her. A new and brutal power has entered the realm of the pacific Indians. The power is the power of greed; everyone is infected.

Jamie Lockhart's sole interest is the accumulation of capital. "Take first and ask afterward" is our hero's motto. Rosamond, damsel that she appears to be, becomes Jamie's wife and then the mistress of a mansion more lavish than the one her wicked stepmother coveted. And Salome herself is the essence of greed: "We must cut down more of the forest, and stretch away the fields until we grow twice as much cotton, twice as much tobacco. For the land is there for the taking, and I say, if it can be taken, take it." It is little wonder that the Indians of history, faced with this plague of human locusts, reacted with violence to defend themselves but were overcome.

The second reckoning of the novella is the Indians' twilight; they appear weary and decimated, faint shadows of their former "blazing" selves. They have been exhausted in the struggle against the intruders; for them "sleep had come to be sweeter than revenge." When Salome insults the sun, the Indians' divinity, they hesitate to strike her dead. In former times she would have been executed on the spot. "And Clement, from where he was bound, saw the sad faces of the Indians, like the faces of feverish children, and said to himself, 'The savages have only come the sooner to their end; we will come to ours too. Why have I built my house, and added to it? The planter will go after the hunter, and the merchant after the planter, all having their day.' "

Clement sees, in the faces of the Indians, the human fate of extinction. They are, to him, just another group of humans overtaken by change, as he himself will be overtaken. He is the planter about to give place to the merchant, Jamie. A stronger, more brutally efficient force is always wresting control of the present. The Indians and Clement become relics of the past.

The town and the Indians are reminders of the universe that resists the fastening of a human dream to a real wilderness. This is Clement's perspective. Through the novella he has resisted and doubted change and "progress," quixotically trying to preserve his illusions in a world of real and treacherous forces. He is an innocent, like Don Quixote. But his dream is not romantic chivalry. He dreams of harmony, of a pastoral gentleness, of the kind of mutually beneficial and cooperative human community that lured Hawthorne's Coverdale and for a brief time held off his skepticism.

Clement Musgrove is a character in a cast of cartoons. He is round and the others are flat. He is the work of a novelist; the others are the work of the skilled caricaturist. The other members of the pioneer cast can be defined as stereotypes—the hero, the damsel, the wicked stepmother—but Clement must be dealt with as a person of considerable dimension. He enters with the naïve innocence of Don Quixote or Candide; and he grows, through the development of his conscience, memory, and foresight, toward an encompassing vision. Like the Indians, he is pushed aside by time and change.

While the pioneers around him are ruthlessly taking everything that is not nailed down, Clement cannot, or will not, push himself over the psychological threshold that bars him from adding to his possessions. His conscience is the barrier. Salome's insistent greed dismays him: "To encompass so much as that is greedy. . . . It would take too much of time and the heart's energy." Ownership, for Clement, is a matter of conscience; it is more emotionally complex than the mere piling up of land or loot. But such is the malleable condition of his conscience, as it grows, that he bends to Salome's desire and adds to his plantation, hoping, with a fair amount of self-delusion, that each new demand will be her last.

The toll of pioneering into the wilderness is collected from Clement's heart. The Indians were cleared away with the trees of the forest; and the guilt of that offense lodges in Clement's heart. The Indians and the forest are the outright victims of pioneering. Clement is a victim in a more comare the outright victims of pioneering. Clement is a victim in a more complicated way. He carries the burden of guilt; the more he sees, the heavier the burden becomes.

There is no mistaking the quality of naïve vulnerability in Clement when he appears. He steps from the riverboat, during the flush times of Rodney, carrying in plain sight, "a bag of gold and many presents." His riches are protected with nothing more formidable than his own "tight grip," even though the place is swarming with bandits. We also learn that he has sold his tobacco for a "fair price" at a time when fortunes were to be made. But Clement is not a tycoon, not a wheeler-dealer, and not apparently motivated by the desire for great profit. He lives up to his name; he is a fair, clement man, avoiding extremes of profit and poverty. But he lives in a world of wild extremes. And, as if to underline the contrast between his clemency and the wide-open world of the frontier, a fabulous storm whirls into Rodney minutes after Clement debarks.

Another facet of Clement's guilelessness is his gullibility. Rejecting the deceit and deviousness in plain sight (a series of innkeepers whose missing ears signify punishment for past crimes), Clement is duped by dishonesty that he fails to see. At last he meets an innkeeper with both ears intact, but he fails to notice how those ears perk up like a rabbit's at the tempting prospect of such a rich and unsuspecting customer as himself. Clement, to his grief, pronounces this innkeeper an honest man.

A shrewder, more worldly person would not automatically accept someone at face value; he would have the imagination of evil to suspect duplicity. But Clement's imagination is, as yet, innocent of such things. He prefers his illusion of worldly wisdom to a real and vigilant cynicism. In choosing Jamie Lockhart to hear his life history, Clement is again guided by face value: "He [Jamie] was remarkably amiable to see. But by his look, nobody could tell what he would do." Not surprisingly, Jamie entirely misses the import of Clement's story. He listens as a gentleman would, but his bandit's brain all the time calculates how much Clement might be worth.

Clement's story shows that his heart feels the costs of pioneering, in sorrow, loss, general estrangement, and that his mind is beginning to be puzzled about the reasons. There has been a great enduring separation in Clement's life. "The reason I ever came is forgotten now," he says, as the preface to his history. "I know I am not a seeker after anything," he continues, "and ambition in this world never stirred my heart once. Yet it seemed as if I was caught up by what came over the others, and they were the same. There was a great tug at the whole world, to go down over the edge, and one and all we were changed into pioneers, and our hearts and our lonely homelessness of the displaced person. Clement, without ambition, without the motivation to seek, to pile up, is an alien in the pioneer life.

Clement is only aware of the pain of dislocation, not of its causes. His memory preserves the name of former comfort and peace—Amalie. Her name suggests a natural kinship with Clement, but she is also part of the past that Clement has left behind. The temptation to "go home again" is as strong as the memory itself. Clement confesses to Jamie that he often struggles in a dream with the tensions he keeps down while awake: "In the dream, whenever I lie down, then it is the past. When I climb to my feet, then it is the present. And I keep up a struggle not to fall."

Clement is moored to the past, like the town of Rodney and the Indians. But, unlike them, he is tied to a long line that plays him into the future. This is an unusual and complicated situation for a character in a fairy tale. Time is not a real consideration for Mike Fink, Jamie Lockhart, or Rosamond. But Clement is part of the author's concern with change. He is the only character in the novel capable of appreciating, perhaps not intellectually, but intuitively, the expanse of time that will eventually erase all human enterprise. Everyone else is wrapped up in the present.

Jamie Lockhart is full of advice for Clement and tells him that when the going gets deep and heavy, he should discard all his useless moral baggage. "Don't fret over the reason," he says, "for it may have been in stars"; and "Guilt is a burdensome thing to carry about in the heart. I would never bother with it." Clement recognizes the advice; he answers Jamie: "Then you are a man of action . . . a man of the times, a pioneer and a free agent. There is no one to come to you saying 'I want' what you do not want."

For Jamie and his fellow pioneers, the chance to grab the wealth of a lifetime in one stroke—the main chance—is too great to be complicated by intangibles like conscience or the reasons for things. This is the irresistible tug that has drawn the pioneers, through acts of greed and violence, toward the goal. Clement knows better than anyone, being married to Salome, how strong is the desire to take, to exploit, to own what no white man has possessed before. Back in civilization, forms, customs, and laws checked unruly impulses like greed and grandiose schemes of possession. But those checks did not follow the pioneers into the wilderness. The lack of them creates a moral wilderness that baffles Clement as much as the literal one. In such a world, he thinks it better to conserve life's energy than to risk it for loot that, besides being ephemeral, collects a tax from the human heart.

For the pioneer, the past has been left behind. But memory of the past is the keystone of Clement's character. His memory of the little group huddled around a campfire just before the Indians effortlessly penetrate the circle dled around a campfire just before the Indians effortlessly penetrate the circle and burst the illusion of security, reminds him that nothing he gathers around himself for familiarity and protection is as firm or impenetrable as it seems. In time, Clement learns that even his own family circle (Salome, Rosamond, and Jamie) have left him alone, pursuing, each in his or her own way, dreams of wealth and success.

Jamie Lockhart, even though he locks up the heart of the fair Rosamond, has a locked heart himself. He *seems* to change, to see the futility of his acquisitive ways, but the tone of irony makes it probable that he changes only in appearance. It has been Jamie's delusion that he could be both gentleman and robber. He has applied the berry stain disguise and washed it off so many times that he finally reaches a point at which he is caught, half-gentleman and half-robber. Little Harp, whom Welty uses as a dark image of the robber half of Jamie, makes this discovery, forcing Jamie to choose between robber and gentleman. Jamie kills Little Harp. But is the dark side gone forever? Maybe Jamie would like to think so. He goes on to become a wealthy, prominent New Orleans merchant. "[T]he outward transfer from bandit to merchant had been almost too easy to count it a change at all, and he was enjoying all the same success he had ever had. But now, in his heart, Jamie knew that he was a hero and had always been one, only with the power to look both ways and to see a thing from all sides."

Although toads may metamorphose into princes in romance, Jamie's transformation is little more than an outward transfer. Jamie has not been as deeply tested as Clement, whose heart is far more respectable than Jamie's. Jamie has stepped from success to success and never held anything in his heart more complicated or painful "than a dream of true love—something of gossamer and roses." He is the compleat businessman; his satiric foil is Goat, the troll-like bumpkin whose parodies of hard bargaining always result in a self-fleecing.

Jamie is very close in instinct and motto to Solome, herself a sour distillation of envy, greed, and ambition. Salome is obsessed with taking, owning, and displaying. She urges Clement to absorb more land, place it under cultivation, and make it pay. She envies every ounce of attention Rosamond receives, storing up her revenge for a grand climax. She is described as several animals—a cat, a vulturelike, clawed bird—and she looms like a black shadow on the borders of several scenes. The overstating of her wickedness, however, reaches tall-tale proportions early in the novella; the result is that the reader seldom takes her seriously. Who really fears the evil of the "wicked stepmother"?

But Salome should not be taken too lightly, for her kind of evil is special.

It originates in greed and a grudge against the wilderness. The land must be compelled to work for her. She represents the extreme precipitation of the tug that pulled the pioneers into the new lands. In the character of Salome we see the frightening truth of what happens to human beings when the checks of civilization are left behind. Clement sees it also. If the zest to explore the unknown is one of man's noblest activities, then the cold intent to subject the earth to his possession and to make it serve his desires is one of his least noble.

Salome's ultimate dream is "a mansion at least five stories high, with an observatory of the river on top of that, with twenty-two Corinthian columns to hold up the roof." Clement must have been sadly surprised to see Rosamond's happily-ever-after on the shores of Lake Pontchartrain: "a beautiful house of marble and cyprus wood . . . with a hundred slaves." It is more opulent than Salome's dream. The surprise must be all the more aching because Rosamond has always been her father's pet, content to let him think of her as the delicate princess in need of protection and rescue. But she has always been, for the readers, more shrewd than that, and cunning in the way she gets her man. She shows her true colors when she lies to her father about being married to Jamie by a priest. In that moment she uses Clement's innocence as Jamie and Salome had used it.

The last word of the novella, or close to the last, is the last word on Rosamond. Clement is about to return upriver once again with the gold his crop has brought. But Rosamond stays behind, in the city. She is part of the new age that has superseded Clement. The city, the place of doubleness, where vice and beauty live together, is too exotic for Clement. "But the city was splendid, she [Rosamond] said; it was the place to live."

Clement lives an Emersonian maxim: "Our life is an apprenticeship to the truth that around every circle another can be drawn; that there is no end in nature, but every end is a beginning; that there is always another dawn risen on mid-noon, and under every deep a lower deep opens" ("Circles"). He lives it in his heart, feeling there the unseen, outer circles. He has seen in the faces of the Indians pride and triumph brought down to impotence and weariness as time runs out. And he accepts himself as an end and Jamie as a beginning in the constant revolution of time. But "he was an innocent of the wilderness . . . and this was his good." It is essential to his innocence that he remain clement, leaving action to the Salomes and Jamies, violent resistance to the Indians. His way is contemplation.

In his moment of private reckoning, Clement sees each individual tree and bird, and also the continuity of all things. Time bothers him most persistently: "What is the place and time?" The trees grow straight and tall,

birds sing from the branches, everything seems to be harmonious and ordered. But there is a menacing presence that threatens the tranquility.
"Across this floor, slowly and softly and forever moving into profile, is always
a beast, one of a procession, weighted low with his burning coat, looking
from the yellow eye set in his head." A beast like that of impending chaos
in Yeats' "The Second Coming" haunts Clement's vision. He worries, like
Yeats, that the way of the world is down from order, accelerating toward
chaos.

Clement's thoughts and emotions in his moment of choice are complex;
he is deeply troubled by a sense of the contradictions in things and people.
The mutability of all things haunts his consciousness, yet all around him he
sees people living in ignorance of it. Clement's personal outlook, in this
respect, is a more conscious and reflective version of the outlook of the
Indians. His special relationship with them is not an accident. He knows
what they only feel—their inescapable doom in the waves of white pioneers.
And he knows further that the tug pulling the pioneers will result in nothing
more permanent than the life the Indians had. Rodney is the place to verify
that.

Two words clash in Clement's vision; the old will be destroyed. The
beast with the single yellow eye is the harbinger of the new, forever revolving
into the present. The beast means to Clement that the end point of progress
is not a perfect pastoral Eden on earth. How can that be the culmination,
Clement must think, even though the dreams and hopes and images dangling
before the pioneers are the most desirable the human imagination can create?
How can this pioneering adventure end in idyll when it is based on doubleness, on greed that is called a noble errand, on ambition that shuts out
every human consideration except the piling up of fantastic gain?

> But the time for cunning has come. . . . And my time is over,
> for cunning is of a world I will have no part in. Two long ripples
> are following down the Mississippi behind the approaching som-
> nolent eyes of the alligator. And like the tenderest deer, a band
> of copying Indians poses along the bluff to draw us near them.
> Men are following men down the Mississippi, hoarse and arrogant
> by day, wakeful and dreamless by night at the unknown landings.
> A trail leads like a tunnel under the roof of this wilderness.
> Everywhere the traps are set. Why? And what kind of time is
> this, when all is first given, then stolen away?

Just as Coverdale and Carraway attended to the romantic dream of
earthly perfection, until the means of getting it proved invalid and false,

cost to the human heart. To continue to pursue, he would have had to assume a doubleness toward himself and the world, taking what was there while pretending it was free.

The Robber Bridegroom accommodates its elements of myth, folk tale, legend, fantasy, blood violence, and historical fact within a theme of the spoiled pastoral—paradise dreamed, desired, lost. Hawthorne made use of such a theme in *The Blithedale Romance*; the ideal society desired by the communitarian reformers was contaminated and finally spoiled by the humans involved. Fitzgerald struck the same note of disenchantment in *The Great Gatsby*; whatever glowing possibilities the new world held out were poisoned the moment man entered to take possession of his dream.

Welty has taken great care in the selection and composition of *The Robber Bridegroom*. Choosing the town of Rodney as the place for the tale and modeling the Indians on the Natchez are conspicuous choices that deepen the story's theme and meaning. The cycles of the plot and the frequency of individual circle images prove close and delicate attention to construction. There is more here than simple good fun with a few childhood fairy tales.

The integration of society called for in the resolution of a comedy is present only in appearance. Happy-ever-after is not a future in the real world, only in fairy tales. Jamie and Rosamond do live happily and prosperously ever after. But their opulent establishment recalls the grand and futile obsession of Salome.

The time has brought change. The pioneer has given way to the middleman, as the Indians had been forced aside by the pioneers. It is as Clement feared. His dream of a paradise of integrity, where appearance and reality are united, where cunning is nonexistent, has vanished. Welty seems to be saying that the dream of a pastoral paradise on earth is always one step ahead of the dreamers; it is, sadly, only possible in a dream world removed from contact with human flesh and imperfections. But still worth dreaming. Alfred Kazin stated this well in his review. Our myths are always sparking our hopes; reality is always dousing them: "Every myth we tell each other today, or try to restore, is only the symbol for our own longing, and turns upon itself. Not the smallest part of Miss Welty's rather exquisite achievement is the skill with which she reminds us that the enchanted forest is for us to recapture—and is forever dead."

The real hero of *The Robber Bridegroom* is Clement. Like Don Quixote, he wrestles with evil valiantly, and loses. Clement, more authentically than Jamie, has the power to "see a thing from all sides." But seeing the doubleness in all things, he does not attack it; nor does he act as if it were not there. Clement acknowledges the vital necessity of mystery (the limits to human

Clement acknowledges the vital necessity of mystery (the limits to human understanding), most of which goes out of the world as time and arrogant human meddling have their way.

Clement, as a hero, retreats. But he has won an integrating vision; he has learned through physical and emotional trial the continuity of time and its concentration in the moment. The technique of *The Robber Bridegroom* works to furnish that moment. The Natchez and the town of Rodney haunt the background as reminders of time past, of human culture and industry done, wiped out, or simply and willy-nilly abandoned. In the foreground the bustle of civilization continues under the spell of progress and profit. But Clement, knowing intuitively the lesson of the past, has seen the future: time is a continuous cycle; the moment of unscaled human vision is the only true stability.

RAAD CAWTHON

Eudora Welty's South Disdains Air Conditioning: An Interview

Eudora Welty's house has a feel about it of an earlier time.

The source of that easy feel is difficult to place. Maybe the gentle light brings it in as it filters into the large rooms through open, wide windows. Or perhaps it wafts in on the un-air-conditioned breeze, cool for September, which stirs the draperies.

The breeze has the mild chill of those first days, between the dog days and Indian summer, when you know the season is changing and another year is dying. It is a time of year Miss Welty loves.

"I love to be in touch with the seasons," she says, gazing at the oak which shades her front windows. "People simply cannot understand that I don't air-condition, but this is so lovely. The other day between the time I was fixing to go to the Jitney and the time I left I counted six pairs of robins on the lawn. I said to myself, 'The season is changing.' "

Eudora Welty, the 73-year-old literary treasure of the state of Mississippi, is about as Southern as you can get. Her fiction, heavily flavored with Southern scenes and personalities, has brought her every major literary award this country can offer, including a Pulitzer Prize. The people who fill her numerous short stories and five novels populate a portrait of the South as accurate and indelible as any since William Faulkner's.

And Eudora Welty's voice is as Southern as the Delta is flat. It's bright, pleasant, and precise. It sounds like pear honey tastes.

Born on North Congress Street in Jackson on April 13, 1909, Miss Welty was raised here. Her father, a business executive with Lamar Life

From *Conversations with Eudora Welty*. © 1982 by *The Clarion-Ledger*. The University Press of Mississippi, 1984. Originally entitled "Eudora Welty's South Disdains Air Conditioning."

Insurance Co., chose Jackson to move to from Ohio. Her mother, a West Virginia native, was a teacher.

The house where she was born still stands. It is the pretty two-story one on the west of Congress Street which was recently renovated as an architect's office.

During her childhood Miss Welty's father, the son of a farmer, decided to move to the country. He chose a lot across from Belhaven College and built a sturdy burgher's house of stucco and brick. Miss Welty, who has never married, still lives there, working at a desk in front of her upstairs bedroom windows, shopping at a nearby grocery, supporting the local arts scene, puttering in her yard, and always writing.

"My friends are very protective of me," she says.

At other times Miss Welty has termed herself "locally underfoot."

The house is large and comfortable but still modest. Easy chairs dot the living room and books, mostly English novels right now, are stacked on a table beside one of them. A large portrait of Miss Welty, dressed in yellow, is framed on an easel in the dining room door. The overall atmosphere is of genteel ease.

Ever since they began taking notice of her, critics have written about Miss Welty's remarkable "ear," her uncanny ability to put onto paper the way people actually speak. It is a gift which few writers have. And Miss Welty's virtuosity with it is matched by only one other, the late Flannery O'Connor.

"When I was young, maybe four or five years old, my family would go driving on Sunday afternoon. My mother told me I used to get up in the backseat and sit between her and one of her friends. I would get myself all fixed and then say, 'OK, start talking.' I suppose I learned a lot about dialogue that way."

Miss Welty looks out the windows and smiles. Her white hair is cut short and curls around the top of her ears. With blue eyes and an animated smile she has in person a look which is softer, more at ease than any photograph of her I have ever seen. Indeed, she does not like cameras and is uncomfortable in front of one.

But in conversation Miss Welty relaxes. Her eyes sparkle. Caught up on a thought, she sits deep in her chair and drapes a long arm above her head. Even though her fame reaches far beyond the parochial confines of Mississippi it is obvious Miss Welty has given much thought to the literary richness of the South where she and so many writers took root.

"I was very fortunate to grow up here. I think anyone who grew up in the South was fortunate, particularly writers. In the South the story is an integral part of life. Stories are just told. You get a sense of narrative.

"One of the most marvelous things is hearing all these stories and getting a sense of family and continuity. It is the world of memory. Through all these stories everything that happens can be kept and repeated and maybe understood later on.

"Because of all that I feel I am a link in a chain. Somehow I am a part of all this, more than an individual."

The first two years of Miss Welty's college life were spent at the Mississippi State College for Women in Columbus. She went there from the sheltered life of a small-town Jackson and discovered deversity unlike any she had known before.

"When I went to MSCW there were a lot of girls there, four to a room. It was crowded. I remember it was my first exposure to people from across the state. The different voices! There was the difference in the way the people from the hill country spoke and those from the Delta.

"I loved it. I used to sit up at night and just listen to the voices coming down the hall. I would try to see if I could tell what part of the state the girls were from by their different voices."

It was a key link in her education as a writer.

Miss Welty took the memory of those voices with her when she left Mississippi for the University of Wisconsin and on to study business at Columbia University in New York.

After her schooling, where she learned to type "so I could be a secretary and make a living," she came back to Jackson. The Great Depression had a strangle hold on the South. About the same time Miss Welty's father died and she took a job as a photographer with the Works Progress Administration. Her project was Mississippi and she traveled it from end to end, taking pictures of its people and listening to their stories.

It was a short course in her native state.

"It showed me another side of the state and of life that I hadn't seen. I think it was good for me."

Her first book of short stories, *A Curtain of Green*, was finished shortly after her job as a WPA photographer ran out.

"I have always written. I love the story. I love to write.

"I've written everywhere, on trains and in motels. All I ask for to write is privacy. And sometimes the only way to get privacy is to leave home.

"As a matter of fact I have found the anonymity of a motel to be a good place to write."

The richness of her imagination and her sure knowledge of place takes precedence over monotonous motel decor.

So, almost wherever she is, Miss Welty spends the early morning hours writing. "The earlier the better," she says. "I have always had more ideas than I could write. I wake up now ready to go."

It is a great gift to a writer to have the love of language, the memory, and the stamina Eudora Welty obviously has. But the gifts were honed for years before she saw her work published. For anyone it must have been a time of frustration, but she never faltered.

"No, it didn't surprise me that I became a writer.

"Perhaps, if I had been more aware of how difficult it can be, I would have been more self-conscious. And if I had been self-conscious, I could have given up. You know, I published in some little magazine for the first six years I was writing but I didn't get any money for it.

"The editors in the big magazines were always encouraging. They would write me back and say 'We like your story but we don't think it's right for us at this time.' "

She pauses and laughs.

"Well, I guess everybody who has ever gotten a rejection slip knows what they say."

Her rejection slips could have filled a well. Perhaps it is indicative of her heart that Miss Welty, instead of dwelling on the rejection, thought of the "nice things" the editors said and kept writing.

Now she is acknowledged as one of the finest writers of our time. Magazines solicit her work and the *New York Times* asks her to review books. Her short stories have been collected and some of her novels staged as plays or opera.

And all the time she keeps working.

"I guess I am superstitious about my work. It doesn't exist in any way until it's finished. A work of fiction is a whole, it's not a piece of knitting. I never show anyone what I've done until it's finished. Never. Never. Never. If I did it would cease to be mine."

Miss Welty looks at the floor and shakes her head. It is as if she is reciting a personal, irrevokable commandment.

"The moment I mail a story away when no one has ever read it is the time when I feel the best. When I put it in the mail I'm elated. But by that night or within the next few hours I am in complete despair. I suppose part of that is being physically tired. Then, when I hear from my agent or editor and they like it I find that the story has changed its character."

She pauses.

"It's as if it's gone down the mail slot at the post office and you can't reach your arm down and get it.

"At that time it ceases to be yours anymore."

She stares across the coffee table with her bright blue eyes. Then, with a wave of her hand, Miss Welty sweeps the vision away.

"I guess that I am just a terribly emotional writer," she says.

"Whenever I get the galley proofs on anything I think, 'Oh, this is horrible. This can't have been done by me, there are too many mistakes.'

"But as I've gotten older I've learned to trust myself. I've learned to think that I've done the best I can. I know now that if I had it back again I would just ruin it.

"What I try to do is communicate from the writer's imagination to the reader's imagination. I don't write for anyone special . . . I write for the sake of the story. The story is everything. I am just the instrument."

There is a sudden stop to the conversation.

"Oh, my goodness!" Miss Welty says. She puts her right palm over her heart. "Don't write that. That sounds so self-righteous. It sounds like *I am* the instrument."

As she makes the statement Miss Welty twirls the index finger on her left hand toward the ceiling and laughs.

"I don't mean it that way at all."

What Miss Welty means is that she tells us about ourselves by refining and distilling the minute elements of our nature. Her writing does not chronicle our temporal history but instead records our mores and our many voices. Her writing is art of the highest order in that it helps us understand who we are.

Miss Welty's concern is not with the ticking of earthbound clocks but with the mumurs of the human heart.

And nowhere did she find so much to distill as in the world of Central Mississippi.

"I'm glad I grew up in Jackson when it was small and manageable. It's good for a writer to have a world where you know it all, where everything is accessible by foot or bicycle. I don't think we are like that anymore.

"I invent my characters from other people or from combining a number of people. My characters come from human beings. You can't invent emotions but you can have characters carry them out in a dramatic way."

As we talk we walk outside. As Miss Welty walks toward her side yard she laments the harsh toll the heat has taken on her camellias and azaleas. Running across the front of the house the porch turns and ends in a side porch open to the elements. She stops in its shade.

"I screened this porch with the first money I ever got from a magazine story. $42 and some cents. But (hurricane) Camille got the screen and I couldn't afford to have it replaced. They wanted something like $400 to rescreen it so I just had the old screen carried away."

The mid-day sun is bright and beginning to slant westward. Shadows are growing longer. The talk turns to current best-sellers and how some writers produce books in the same efficient, calculated way McDonald's produces hamburgers.

Miss Welty tells of reading a profile in a national magazine concerning a popular female author who sleeps in false eyelashes so she won't have to apply them before going on camera at early-morning talk shows.

"Can you imagine that?" she says. "It's frightening. I would do the worst sort of manual labor before I would live like that."

You can almost see her cringe. It is difficult to imagine Miss Welty even owning false eyelashes. She stops and shakes her head.

"When I read that I thought, 'Is this what writing is all about, sleeping in false eyelashes?' "

No, Miss Welty, we both know it's not. Besides, it would be a shame to hide those baby blues.

PATRICIA MEYER SPACKS

Gossip and Community in Eudora Welty

Eudora Welty, writing mainly of the experience of white Southerners, uses and merges mythologizing talk about past and present, exploiting both comic and serious possibilities. Reading through *The Collected Stories*, one encounters a series of distinctive and powerful voices, voices participating often in shifting patterns of conversation, voices that sometimes speak directly to the reader, sometimes talk to themselves. The stories contain diverse characters, settings, and events; although theme and character link some, others bear no obvious connection to one another. Yet, reading them together, one feels in touch with a community. The voices comment on one another, weaving a rich linguistic texture and affirming the necessity and the vitality and the creativity of talking about people.

Not that each voice is in itself attractive. "Petrified Man," from Welty's first published collection (1941), begins, " 'Reach in my purse and git me a cigarette without no powder in it if you kin, Mrs. Fletcher, honey,' said Leota to her ten o'clock shampoo-and-set customer. 'I don't like no perfumed cigarettes.' " The vulgarity and self-centeredness of utterance, the coziness of tone dominate the entire story. Leota and Mrs. Fletcher speak mainly of other people; from their conversation emerges the tale of Mrs. Pike ("Honey, 'cute' ain't the word for what she is. I'm tellin' you, Mrs. Pike is attractive. She has her a good time. She's got a sharp eye out, Mrs. Pike has." Mrs. Pike's "sharp eye" uncovers in the petrified man of a circus sideshow a criminal wanted for raping four women in California; Leota's enthusiasm for her and her small son markedly diminishes when Mrs. Pike collects five hundred dollars' reward. But plot has relatively little to do with the story's

From *Gossip*. © 1985 by Patricia Meyer Spacks. Alfred A. Knopf, 1985. Originally entitled "The Living Breath of Event."

comedy. Plot functions to reveal character—which is to say, plot uncovers what voice leaves implicit. Leota's self-absorption, vulgarity, and superficiality play themselves out in her responses to shifting circumstances as she discusses Mrs. Fletcher's pregnancy (and the absorbing question of how she herself found out about it) and her relationship with Mrs. Pike, whom she first admires for her skill at coping with social exigencies and then envies and dislikes for the same skill, expressing her rage finally by paddling Mrs. Pike's little boy, who runs away yelling, "If you're so smart, why ain't you rich?"—a profoundly appropriate question.

Talking about other people, Leota reveals herself. Greedy and heartless, she cannot preserve her façade of amiability. She gets her comeuppance in comically exact fashion: nothing could punish Leota more effectively than missing a chance at money. The story, despite its dazzling precision of detail, makes the beautician representative of her type. Magnified into significance by the exactness of her rendering, Leota in all her triviality plays a vivid part in Welty's drama of the South.

In the culture Welty evokes, people talk constantly about one another, generating legends even of the present. Present and past often merge, for Welty as for Faulkner. Miss Katie Rainey, "the old lady that watches the turn of the road" until her death, figures in "The Wanderers" (1949) as one who not only sees but hears. The voices she hears come from her imagination. They tell contemporary truth, yet belong to the past; they speak of human recurrence. She waits for her daughter, past forty now, and she listens:

> Waiting, she heard circling her ears like the swallows beginning, talk about lovers. Circle by circle it twittered, church talk, talk in the store and post office, vulgar man talk possibly in the barbershop. Talk she could never get near now was coming to her.
> "So long as the old lady's alive, it's all behind her back."
> "Daughter wouldn't run off and leave her, she's old and crippled."
> "Left once, will again."
> "That fellow Mabry's been taking out his gun and leaving Virgie a bag of quail every other day. Anybody can see him go by the back door."
> "I declare.". . .
> "Oh, sure. Fate Rainey's a clean shot, too."
> "But ain't he heard?"
> Not Fate Rainey at all; but Mr. Mabry. It was just that the talk Miss Katie heard was in voices of her girlhood, and some times they slipped.

Fate Rainey is Miss Katie's dead husband; Mr. Mabry is courting her daughter. Her own experience and her daughter's merge as she listens to the voices of her community, voices of fantasy. "I been by myself all day," she tells her daughter, Virgie: yet this world hardly allows isolation. The community and its voices interpenetrate all experience. Miss Katie expresses truth to herself in the guise of imagined gossip.

The constant impingement on the individual of the community's voices and judgments becomes Virgie's preoccupation when left alone by her mother's death. The account of rituals and ceremonies surrounding the death, of people coming to the house of mourning and of what they say, occupies much of the story. Then Virgie, finally alone, drives to a neighboring village, looks at a cemetery, sits in the rain. Her meditations recall other people's insistent opinions. She remembers a man buried in the cemetery who "lived in another part of the world," leaving for a time, keeping his own secrets, yet never avoiding persistent assessment by those of his home place. Virgie avoids an encounter with Mr. Mabry, walking in the rain, who fails to see her because she wishes not to be seen. "She watched him march by. Then she was all to herself." She thinks about the extreme difficulty, perhaps the impossibility, of being all to oneself. Remembering a picture of Perseus with the head of Medusa, she thinks about that too. "Cutting off the Medusa's head was the heroic act, perhaps, that made visible a horror in love, Virgie thought—the separateness." Horror, yet also goal. With a black woman holding a hen, Virgie sits under a tree in the rain. "Then she and the old beggar woman, the old black thief, were there alone and together in the shelter of the big public tree, listening to the magical percussion, the world beating in their ears. They heard through falling rain the running of the horse and bear, the stroke of the leopard, the dragon's crusty slither, and the glimmer and the trumpet of the swan."

Both alone and together at the story's end, Virgie and the black woman "hear" natural creatures—not so natural either, in the rural South: animals of legend, rather, imaginable out of literary tradition—in much the same way that Virgie's mother has earlier "heard" voices of the community. Isolation, separation are temporary constructions at best. In fictive isolation, the woman conjures up the alternative community of an imagined animal creation. Those surrounding Virgie in her everyday life are busybodies, compulsive interferers with and talkers about others; they will not leave her alone. Yet to live alone would be, after all, a horror. The gossip that plagues Virgie, the town's compulsive interest in the affairs of others, also affirms necessary connection: an arrangement of things superior to any imaginable alternative. Even the vision of running animals in their beauty and freedom gains intensity of being shared, if only silently.

In "Kin" (1955), Welty investigates the ties of family. These too flourish in talk about others, talk weaving a web of story that binds relatives and descendants of the story's subjects.

> "On purpose, I think she fell [in the well]," continued Kate. "Knowing there were plenty to pull her out. That was her contribution to Cousin Eva's wedding celebrations, and snitching a little of *her* glory. . . ."
>
> "There's such a thing as being unfair, Kate," said her mother. "I always say, *poor* Sister Anne."
>
> "*Poor* Sister Anne, then."
>
> "And I think Dicey just *thinks* she remembers it because she's heard it."
>
> "Well, at least she had something to be poor about!" I said irrepressibly. "Falling in the well, and being an old maid, that's two things!"
>
> Kate cried, "Don't rock so headlong!"
>
> "Maybe she even knew what she was about. Eva's Archie Fielder got drunk every whipstitch for the rest of his life," said Aunt Ethel.
>
> "Only tell me this, somebody, and I'll be quiet," I said. "What poor somebody's Sister Anne was she to begin with?"

The narrator, Dicey Hastings, a young woman visiting Mississippi from the North, has lived in this community as a child. She comments, early in her story, that "Aunt Ethel and Kate, and everybody I knew here, lived as if they had never heard of anywhere else, even Jackson." The dialogue about "poor Sister Anne" exemplifies the kind of conversation that preoccupies Aunt Ethel and Kate and that fascinates Dicey, even though she does not always know or remember its characters. A steady stream of reminiscence, speculation, and genealogizing recalls past scandals, softens past tragedies, recapitulates lost pleasures. It consolidates the participants' conviction that they occupy the center of the universe.

This talk helps to orient Dicey, a "double first cousin" of Kate. As cultural myths locate their people—Greeks, American Indians, Norse, whatever—in the universe, explaining why things are as they are, so this chatter locates each individual in a universe of "kin." It tells Dicey where she belongs. When she and Kate go out in the country, to visit ancient Uncle Felix and poor Sister Anne, they go in the knowledge of family story (rumor, gossip, memory). A crowd of people occupy the house; the girls assume Uncle Felix has died. In fact Sister Anne has invited an itinerant photographer to take pictures of all comers in the parlor; as a reward, she will receive a free photograph of herself. The girls talk to Uncle Felix in a cluttered back room. He thinks himself at a battle of the past; he gives Dicey a note arranging an assignation with someone unknown, someone probably long dead. The photographer leaves at the same time as the girls. Dicey comments, "I felt the secret pang behind him—I know I did feel the cheat he had found and left in the house, the helpless, asking cheat. I felt it more and more, too strongly." Then the cousins fall into gales of helpless, unaccountable laughter. Recovering, they agree in a negative judgment of Sister Anne: "She's common."

The "helpless, asking cheat" in the house is Sister Anne, desperately trying to hold what she has never in fact possessed. "We're losing him fast," she says of Uncle Felix, adding, "But oh, I can't stand for you all to go! Stay—stay!" A voice from the porch says, as the girls run away, "It seems to me that things are moving in too great a rush." The effort to make everyone and everything "stay," to arrest the rapid passage of time that has reduced Uncle Felix to senility, helps to account for Sister Anne's interest in the photographer. She tries to make herself beautiful for him, but she has never been beautiful; she tries to keep the girls, but they have never been with her; she insists on her integral share in a family which has long ago, by its humorous, reminiscent gossip, judged her and found her wanting: "common." At the end of the girls' fit of laughter, Dicey says, of "Aunt Beck," to whom Kate has referred, "I don't remember her." Kate responds, "But she wouldn't *let* you forget. She *made* you remember her!" Characters inhabit the family story as though by force of their own wills. But in fact this story, like all gossip's stories, takes shape by the power of collective standards and assumptions. Dicey may claim to have forgotten Aunt Beck, but the aunt is remembered nonetheless: she *belongs*, identifying herself with natural beauty (she gives people flowers) even as Sister Anne connects herself with the artificial scenery of the photographer.

"Kin" hints exclusionary possibilities in what I am calling mythic gossip, the kind that solidifies the traditions of a family or a wider group. Sister Anne emerges as a character unattractive in every way, but the characterization of her as a "helpless, asking cheat" suggests pathos underlying and perhaps generating her unattractiveness. Is she excluded because unattractive, or unattractive because excluded? She epitomizes the decay of a family denying its losses through the stories it tells itself. Dicey feels sufficiently an insider to enjoy conspiratorial laughter with her cousin, but at the end of the story she thinks longingly of her Northern fiancé. She needs, after all, to escape; she feels the airlessness of the myth. In other stories, the confinement of communal myth. In other stories, the confinement of communal myth can seem a horror. "The Whole World Knows," for instance, tells a tragic tale through the consciousness of one of its protagonists—a consciousness including awareness of what "the whole world" knows and says. The summary of town opinion issues from Ran's imagination; these undifferentiated voices resemble those heard by Miss Katie Rainey.

> He walked out on her and took his clothes down to the other end of the street. Now everybody's waiting to see how soon he'll go back. They say Jinny MacLain invites Woody out there to eat, a year younger than she is, remember when they were born. Invites, under her mama's nose. Sure, it's Woodrow Spights she invites. Who else in Morgana would there be for Jinny Stark after Ran, with even Eugene MacLain gone? She's kin to the Nesbitts. They don't say when it started, can anybody tell? At the Circle, at Miss Francine's, at Sunday School, they say, they say she will marry Woodrow; Woodrow'd jump at it but Ran will kill somebody first. . . . He used to be sweet but too much devil in him from Time was, that's Ran. He'll do something bad. He won't divorce Jinny but he'll do something bad.

Ran, who has left his wife, Jinny, because of her adultery, tells his own story; the narrative derives from his consciousness. His awareness of how the town incorporates his misery into its legend of itself, a legend in which everyone is pre-classified, by age and kin and personal history—this awareness intensifies his suffering. Although Ran belongs to the community from which the talk issues, he feels excluded by the irrelevance of that community's judgments to his actual feelings. The story constructed by the town's gossip exists side by side with actual events, never touching, in spite of the fact that the story includes things that have really happened. But gossip at this level concerns itself not with emotions, but only with happenings. The very power of its myths can make it intolerable.

The clearest association between gossip and myth emerges in "Asphodel" (1943). Three old maids (Cora, Phoebe, Irene) on a picnic recall the story of the ruined house, Asphodel, near which they eat their meal, and of the people associated with that house. The language of "Asphodel" has a dignified, distant ring, as far as possible from that of gossip. "They pressed at the pomegranate stains on their mouths. And then they began to tell over Miss Sabina's story, their voices serene and alike: how she looked, the legend of her beauty when she was young, the house where she was born and what happened in it, and how she came out when she was old, and her triumphal way, and the pitiful end when she toppled to her death in a dusty place where she was a stranger, that she had despised and deplored."

The three old maids tell much of the story, their quoted language as stylized as the narrator's. From one point of view, this tale of loss centers on mortality rather than the immortality associated with the flower of the house's name and the narrative's title. Yet it also speaks of permanence, and the women who relate past events, telling over to each other a story long known, create immortality they fail to recognize. The story for them "was only part of memory now," but it is narrative as well as memory: a form of preservation. Their role has always demanded that they speak the community's happenings. When Don McInnis is first unfaithful to his wife, Sabina, " 'We told the news,' said Cora. 'We went in a body up the hill and into the house, weeping and wailing, hardly daring to name the name or the deed.' " When the three of them hear that McInnis "was running away to Asphodel . . . and taking the woman," they go together to tell Miss Sabina. Sabina whips her husband out of the house. That night Asphodel burns; the old maids run and tell Sabina, "and she was gratified—but from that moment remote from us and grand. And she laid down the law that the name of Don McInnis and the name of Asphodel were not to cross our lips again." Naming and telling: these crucial acts belong to the chorus of women. Thus the women solidify the tradition of their place. Sabina, as they describe her, only hears and knows news; she does not tell it. "All news was borne to her first, and she interrupted every news-bearer. 'You don't have to tell me: I know. The woman is dead. The child is born. The man is proved a thief.' "

"Asphodel" concerns itself with power. Don McInnis, from the beginning, embodies a force of nature. Sabina, compelled to marry him, must also submit to him; but the children born of the union die, as though the wrenching together of incompatible energies in their parents makes their survival impossible. Gradually Sabina, despite her subordinate position, develops her own kind of force. She drives her husband away, she dominates the village. " 'She took her stick and went down the street proclaiming and wielding her power,' said Cora. 'Her power reached over the whole population—white and black, men and women, children, idiots, and animals— even strangers.' " But she will not come to the post office, that center of ordinary human communication. When finally she appears there, she demands her letter, although "Miss Sabina never got a letter in her life. She never knew a soul beyond the town." Then she seizes and tears to shreds the letters of others, and then she drops dead, having attempted to destroy

the emotions and connections she cannot share. As far as the three remem-
berers are concerned, this episode concludes the story. "Here in the bright
sun where the three old maids sat beside their little feast, Miss Sabina's was
an old story, closed and complete." But it has not ended after all. The
apparition of a naked man, "as rude and golden as a lion," drives the old
maids away. They recognize him as Don McInnis. Then a herd of little
goats completes their rout. They appease the goats with the contents of an
untouched picnic basket; they drive away. Welty's story ends in these words:
"But Phoebe laughed aloud as they made the curve. Her voice was soft, and
she seemed to be still in a tender dream and an unconscious celebration—
as though the picnic were not already set rudely in the past, but were the
enduring the intoxicating present, still the phenomenon, the golden day."

This conclusion re-articulates the issue of control. Don McInnis's male
power, the old maids' telling implies, yielded to his wife's female equivalent.
He continued to act out his impulses, but she assumed ascendancy in the
community; McInnis, having disappeared, is assumed to be defeated. Cora,
Phoebe, and Irene, functioning mainly as voices, have control of the story,
thus defining reality. They too embody female power. Because they preserve
communal memory, create communal myth, they serve as repositories of
value. But older myths than they acknowledge also shape reality. Don
McInnis becomes assimilated with Pan; as embodiment of nature, he
triumphs over the confining civilization the old maids represent. Irene denies
that they have seen Don McInnis ("it was a vine in the wind"). Cora re-
asserts female authority. " 'What Miss Sabina wouldn't have given to see
him!' cried Cora at last. 'What she wouldn't have told him, what she wouldn't
have done to him!' " Only Phoebe acknowledges the desirability of trying
to hold on to this too, incorporating this mystery into the preservations of
memory and story.

Like Welty's other stories, this wonderful tale specifies and even glorifies
the tattle of a small town, but it also recognizes (like "The Whole World
Knows," for example) the restrictive effect of such talk. "The Whole World
Knows," for example) the restrictive effect of such talk. The exclusionary
myths of gossip explain the community to itself. As the tone of "Asphodel"
emphasizes, they rapidly become legend. Yet they also limit possibilities of
understanding: although they preserve happening and locate it in a rich
human context, they barely acknowledge interior event. Welty's stories,
celebrating and criticizing small-town gossip, suggest both positive and negative reasons for taking gossip seriously.

Chronology

1909   April 13, Eudora Alice Welty born in Jackson, Mississippi, to Mary Chestina and Christian Webb Welty.

1925   Graduates from Central High School, Jackson.

1925–27   Attends Mississippi State College for Women, Columbus.

1927–29   Receives B.A., University of Wisconsin, Madison.

1930–31   Studies advertising at Columbia University School of Business, New York City.

1931   Her father dies; she returns to Jackson to live.

1931–33   Works on newspapers and for Jackson radio station.

1933–36   Works as publicity agent for the WPA in Mississippi; begins taking photographs of people throughout the state.

1936   WPA work ends. Has a show of photographs in New York City. Publishes first stories: "Death of a Traveling Salesman" and "Magic."

1940   Diarmuid Russell, son of the Irish poet George Russell, becomes her literary agent. Welty attends summer program at Breadloaf.

1941   "A Worn Path" wins second prize, O. Henry Memorial Contest Award. Summer at Yaddo. Publishes *A Curtain of Green*, with an introduction by Katherine Anne Porter.

1942   Publishes *The Robber Bridegroom*. "The Wide Net" wins first prize, O. Henry Memorial Contest Award.

1942–43   Receives Guggenheim Fellowship.

1943   Signs with Harcourt Brace, with John Woodburn as her editor. Publishes *The Wide Net and Other Stories*. "Livvie is Back" wins first prize, O. Henry Memorial Contest Award.

1944   Receives award from the Academy of Arts and Letters. Serves on *New York Times Book Review* staff for six months. Uses pseudonym of Michael Ravenna for reviews of World War II battle reports from Europe, North Africa, and South Pacific.

1946   Publishes *Delta Wedding*.

1947   Lectures at Pacific Northwest Writers' Conference.

1949   Publishes *The Golden Apples*.

1949–50 Receives renewal of Guggenheim Fellowship; travels to England, France, and Italy.

1950   Publishes "Short Stories."

1951   "The Burning" published and wins second prize, O. Henry Memorial Contest Award.

1952   Elected to National Institute of Arts and Letters. Travels to England and Ireland.

1954   Publishes *The Ponder Heart* and *Selected Stories*.

1955   Publishes *The Bride of the Innisfallen*. Receives the William Dean Howells Medal of the Academy of Arts and Letters for *The Ponder Heart*. Travels to Europe; participates in conference on American studies at Cambridge University and delivers lecture, "Place in Fiction."

1956   *The Ponder Heart*, adapted as a play, opens on Broadway.

1958   Honorary Consultant in American Letters, Library of Congress.

1958–59 Receives Lucy Donnelly Fellowship Award from Bryn Mawr College.

1960   Receives Ingram Memorial Foundation Award in Literature.

1962   Publishes "Three Papers on Fiction."

1965   Publishes *Thirteen Stories*, with an introduction by Ruth M. Vande Kieft.

1970   Publishes *Losing Battles*. Receives Edward McDowell Medal.

1971   Publishes *One Time, One Place: Mississippi in the Depression, A Snapshot Album*, with an introduction by herself. Becomes member of the American Academy of Arts and Letters.

1972   Publishes *The Optimist's Daughter*. Receives the National Institute of Arts and Letters Gold Medal.

1973   Receives the Pulitzer Prize for *The Optimist's Daughter*.

1978   Publishes *The Eye of the Story: Selected Essays and Reviews*.

1980   Publishes *The Collected Stories of Eudora Welty*. Receives the National Medal of Literature and the Medal of Freedom Award.

1983   Publishes *One Writer's Beginnings*.

Contributors

HAROLD BLOOM, Sterling Professor of the Humanities at Yale University, is the author of *The Anxiety of Influence*, *Poetry and Repression*, and many other volumes of literary criticism. His forthcoming study, *Freud: Transference and Authority*, attempts a full-scale reading of all of Freud's major writings. A MacArthur Prize Fellow, he is general editor of five series of literary criticism published by Chelsea House.

KATHERINE ANNE PORTER is the author of essays, stories, and novels, including *Ship of Fools* and *Pale Horse, Pale Rider*.

ROBERT PENN WARREN is the author of numerous books of poetry and fiction, including *World Enough and Time*, *The Cave*, and *Incarnations*.

JOHN EDWARD HARDY has taught at Yale, Johns Hopkins, and Notre Dame and is the author of *Man in the Modern Novel* and *The Curious Frame*.

RUTH M. VANDE KIEFT, author of *Eudora Welty*, teaches English at Queens College, City University of New York.

JOYCE CAROL OATES is the author of numerous books of poetry and fiction, including *Crossing the Border* and *The Wheel of Love*.

REYNOLDS PRICE, novelist, poet, and professor at Duke University and The University of North Carolina, Chapel Hill, is the author of *Love and Work* and *The Source of Light*.

MALCOLM COWLEY, professor at Stanford and Cornell, is the author of *The Literary Situation*, *After the Genteel Tradition*, and *Exile's Return*.

WALKER PERCY, novelist, has written *The Moviegoer*, *The Last Gentleman*, and *Love in the Ruins*.

CLEANTH BROOKS, founder of *The Southern Review* and for many years a professor at Yale, is the author of *Understanding Poetry, Modern Poetry and the Tradition*, and *The Well Wrought Urn, a Shaping Joy: Studies in the Writer's Craft*.

DANIELE PITAVY-SOUQUES is a member of the School of Modern Languages at the University of Dijon, France.

SEYMOUR GROSS has taught at Notre Dame and the University of Detroit and is the author of *American Literature Survey* and *Images of the Negro in American Literature*.

MICHAEL KREYLING, author of *Eudora Welty's Achievement of Order*, teaches English at Tulane.

RAAD CAWTHON is a writer and contributor to *The Clarion-Ledger Jackson (Mississippi) Daily News*.

PATRICIA MEYER SPACKS, professor of English at Yale, is the author of *The Female Imagination* and *Gossip*.

Bibliography

Blackwell, Louise. "Eudora Welty: Proverbs and Proverbial Phrases in *The Golden Apples*." *Southern Folklore Quarterly* 30 (December 1966): 332–41.

Boyle, Kay. "Full Length Portrait." *New Republic* 105 (November 24, 1941): 707.

Bryant, J. A. *Eudora Welty*. University of Minnesota Pamphlets on American Writers, no. 66. Minneapolis: University of Minnesota Press, 1968.

Curley, Daniel. "Eudora Welty and the Quondam Obstruction." *Studies in Short Fiction* 5 (Spring 1968): 209–24.

Daniel, Robert. "The World of Eudora Welty." *Hopkins Review* 6 (Winter 1953): 49–58.

Desmond, John F., ed. *A Still Moment: Essays on the Art of Eudora Welty*. Metuchen, N.J.: Scarecrow Press, 1978.

Devlin, Albert J. "Eudora Welty's Historicism: Method and Vision." *Mississippi Quarterly* 30 (Spring 1977): 213–34.

Dollarhide, Louis, and Ann J. Abadie, eds. *Eudora Welty: A Form of Thanks*. Jackson: University Press of Mississippi, 1979.

Eisinger, Chester E. *Fiction of the Forties*. Chicago: The University of Chicago Press, 1963.

Evans, Elizabeth. "Eudora Welty: The Metaphor of Music." *The Southern Quarterly* 20, no. 4 (Summer 1982): 92–100.

Glenn, Eunice. "Fantasy in the Fiction of Eudora Welty." In *Critiques and Essays on Modern Fiction, 1920–1951*, edited by John W. Aldridge. New York: The Ronald Press, 1952.

Gross, Seymour L. "Eudora Welty: A Bibliography of Criticism and Comment." Secretary's News Sheet, Bibliography Society, University of Virginia, no. 45 (April 1960).

Heilman, Robert B. "The Southern Temper." *Hopkins Review* 6 (Fall 1952): 5–15.

Hicks, Granville. "Eudora Welty." *College English* 14 (November 1952): 69–76.

Howard, Zelma Turner. *The Rhetoric of Eudora Welty's Short Stories*. Jackson: University Press of Mississippi, 1973.

Howell, Elmo. "Eudora Welty and the Use of Place in Southern Fiction." *Arizona Quarterly* 28 (Autumn 1972): 248–56.

Idol, John L., Jr. "Edna Earle Ponder's Good Country People." *The Southern Quarterly* 20, no. 3 (Spring 1982): 66–74.

Jones, William M. "Name and Symbol in the Prose of Eudora Welty." *Southern Folklore Quarterly* 22 (December 1958): 173–85.

Kieft, Ruth M. Vande. *Eudora Welty*. New York: Twayne Publishers, 1962.

Kreyling, Michael. *Eudora Welty's Achievement of Order*. Baton Rouge: Louisiana State University Press, 1980.

Messerli, Douglas. "The Problem of Time in Welty's *Delta Wedding*." *Studies in American Fiction* 5 (1977–78): 227–40.

Mississippi Quarterly 26 (Fall 1973). Special Eudora Welty issue.

Morris, Harry C. "Eudora Welty's Use of Mythology." *Shenandoah* 6, no. 2 (Spring 1955): 34–40.

Opit, Kurt. "Eudora Welty: The Order of a Captive Soul." *Critique: Studies in Modern Fiction* 7 (Winter 1964–65): 79–91.

Pei, Lowry. "Dreaming the Other in *The Golden Apples*." *Modern Fiction Studies* 28, no. 3 (Autumn 1982): 415–33.

Prenshaw, Peggy Whitman, ed. *Conversations With Eudora Welty*. Jackson: University Press of Mississippi, 1984.

———. *Eudora Welty: Critical Essays*. Jackson: University Press of Mississippi, 1979.

Ransom, John Crowe. "Delta Fiction." *Kenyon Review* 8 (Summer 1946): 503–7.

Rubin, Louis D., Jr. "Two Ladies of the South." *Sewanee Review* 63 (Autumn 1955): 671–81.

Shenandoah 20 (Spring 1969). Special Eudora Welty issue.

Trilling, Diana. "Fiction in Review." *Nation* 162 (May 11, 1946): 578.

Vickery, John. "William Blake and Eudora Welty's 'Death of a Traveling Salesman.' " *MLN* 76 (November 1961): 625–32.

West, Ray B., Jr. "Three Methods of Modern Fiction: Ernest Hemingway, Thomas Mann, and Eudora Welty." *College English* 12 (January 1951): 193–203.

Acknowledgments

"*A Curtain of Green*" (originally entitled "Introduction") by Katherine Anne Porter from *A Curtain of Green* by Eudora Welty, © 1941 by Eudora Welty. Reprinted by permission.

"Love and Separateness in Eudora Welty" by Robert Penn Warren from *Selected Essays* by Robert Penn Warren, © 1958 by Robert Penn Warren. Reprinted by permission of Random House and the author.

"*Delta Wedding* as Region and Symbol" by John Edward Hardy from *The Sewanee Review* 60, no. 3 (Summer 1952), © 1952, 1980 by the University of the South. Reprinted by permission of the Editor of *The Sewanee Review*.

"The Mysteries of Eudora Welty" by Ruth M. Vande Kieft from *Eudora Welty* by Ruth M. Vande Kieft, © 1962 by Twayne Publishers, Inc. Reprinted by permission of Twayne Publishers, a division of G.K. Hall & Co., Boston.

"The Art of Eudora Welty" by Joyce Carol Oates from *Shenandoah* 20 (Spring 1969), © 1969 by Joyce Carol Oates and Washington and Lee University. Reprinted by permission of the author and the Editor of *Shenandoah*.

"The Onlooker, Smiling: An Early Reading of *The Optimist's Daughter*" by Reynolds Price from *Shenandoah* 20 (Spring 1969), © 1969 by Washington and Lee University. Reprinted by permission of the Editor of *Shenandoah*.

"Three Tributes" (originally entitled "Five Tributes") by Malcolm Cowley, Walker Percy, Robert Penn Warren from *Shenandoah* 20 (Spring 1969), © 1969 by Washington and Lee University. Reprinted by permission of the Editor of *Shenandoah*.

"Eudora Welty and the Southern Idiom" by Cleanth Brooks from *Eudora Welty*: *A Form of Thanks*, edited by Louis Dollarhide and Ann J. Abadie, © 1979 by the University Press of Mississippi. Reprinted by permission.

"Technique as Myth: The Structure of *The Golden Apples*" by Daniele Pitavy-Souques from *Eudora Welty*: *Critical Essays*, edited by Peggy Whitman Prenshaw, © 1979 by the University Press of Mississippi. Reprinted by permission.

"A Long Day's Living: The Angelic Ingenuities of *Losing Battles*" by Seymour Gross from *Eudora Welty*: *Critical Essays*, edited by Peggy Whitman Prenshaw, © 1979 by the University Press of Mississippi. Reprinted by permission.

171

"*The Robber Bridegroom* and the Pastoral Dream" by Michael Kreyling from *Eudora Welty's Achievement of Order*, © 1980 by Louisiana State University Press. Reprinted by permission of the publisher.

"Eudora Welty's South Disdains Air Conditioning: An Interview" (originally entitled "Eudora Welty's South Disdains Air Conditioning") by Raad Cawthon from *Conversations with Eudora Welty*, edited by Peggy Whitman Prenshaw, © 1982 by *The Clarion-Ledger*. Reprinted by permission of *The Clarion-Ledger*, Jackson, Miss.

"Gossip and Community in Eudora Welty" (originally entitled "The Living Breath of Event") by Patricia Meyer Spacks from *Gossip* by Patricia Meyer Spacks, © 1985 by Patricia Meyer Spacks. Reprinted by permission of Alfred A. Knopf, Inc.

Index

36–37, 42–43, 72; structure of, 29, 34, 35–36, 38, 39–40; Studney in, 35, 40; subjectivity in, 30; symbolism in, 29, 30, 33, 34–35, 36, 37–38, 39, 40–41, 42; Tempe in, 72; Troy Flavin in, 30, 31, 33, 36, 38, 39, 40, 41, 42; Virgie Lee in, 36
"Demonstrators, The", 75; blacks in, 73, 74; death in, 73, 74; O. Henry First Prize for, 72; horror in, 74; isolation in, 73; Miss Marcia Pope in, 73; symbolism in, 73; violence in, 73
Denis, character of, 36, 37
Dial, 110
Dialect, Southern: background of, 93–96, 101–2; in *Losing Battles*, 96–97; in *The Optimist's Daughter*, 96; in "The Petrified Man," 96–97, 155; in *The Ponder Heart*, 96; in "Why I Live at the P.O.," 96. *See also* Folk culture, Southern
Dickinson, Emily, Welty compared to, 1
Doc, character of, 25
Dow, Lorenzo, character of: horror and, 52–53; isolation of, 2–4, 5, 22, 23; love and, 51, 52, 53–54, 78, 114; separateness and, 78; Welty compared to, 66
Dreams, theme of, 16, 20; in "First Love," 27, 57; in *The Golden Apples*, 115; in "A Memory," 24, 46–47; in *The Robber Bridegroom*, 141, 144, 145, 146, 147; in "A Still Moment," 53
Dreiser, Theodore, Welty compared to, 20

Easter, character of, 111
Eckhart, Miss, character of: love and, 116, 117; myth of Perseus and, 111; Virgie Rainey and, 115, 116, 117
Eisinger, Chester, 140
Eliot, T. S., 110; influence of, on Welty, 112; Welty compared to, 1
Ellen, character of, 35, 40, 72; George and, 38, 39; isolation of, 30, 37; legend and, 37–38; marriage of, 41

Elvie, character of, 128
Emerson, Ralph Waldo, 119; Welty compared to, 120
Erskine, Albert, influence of, on Welty, 14
Ethel, character of, 158
Etoyle, character of, 122
Eva, character of, 158
Evangeline, Lady, character of, 97

Fairchilds, the, characters of: blacks and, 41, 72; George as the ideal of, 36; Laura McRaven and, 40–41, 42, 43, 77; Robbie Reid and, 31, 36–37; world of, 30, 32, 33–34, 36–37, 38–39
Faulkner, William, Welty compared to, 6, 10, 30, 59, 149, 156
Fay, Ella, character of, 132
Fay, Wanda, character of, 85, 88; description of, 99–100; Laurel McKelva Hand and, 79, 80–81, 82, 83, 86–87
Felix, character of, 158, 159
Fiction, Southern: *Delta Wedding* as atypical of, 30; dialect in, 93–107; O'Connor on, 77; pastoral elements of, 31–32; Welty's as, 77, 155; Welty's views on the roots of, 150–51
Fink, Mike, character of, 135–36, 143
First Love (Turgenev), 76
"First Love": Aaron Burr in, 57; dreams in, 27, 57; isolation in, 22; Joel Mayes in, 22, 27, 57, 59; *Losing Battles* compared to, 129; love in, 57; special world of, 20
Fischer, Ruby, character of, 60
Fitzgerald, F. Scott, Welty compared to, 147
Flaubert, Gustave, 74
Flavin, Troy, character of: Billy Floyd compared to, 41; Cash compared to, 41; engagement of, 36, 38; isolation of, 30, 31; marriage of, 33, 39, 40, 41, 42
"Flowers for Marjorie": death in, 49, 50; Howard in, 48, 49–50; irony in, 49; isolation in, 22; love in, 49; Marjorie in, 48–49